BEYOND AWAKENING

The End of
The Spiritual Search

JEFF FOSTER

NON-DUALITY PRESS

For my family

NON-DUALITY PRESS

6 Folkestone Road Salisbury SP2 8JP United Kingdom

www.non-dualitybooks.com

Copyright © Jeff Foster 2007

First printing September 2007

Cover concept and photography: Sally Bongers and Paul Elliot
Layout: John Gustard

For more information visit:
www.geocities.com/thisispresence/

Isbn 10: 0-9553999-7-1
Isbn 13: 978-0-9553999-7-8

"This slowly drifting cloud is pitiful!
What dreamwalkers we all are!
Awakened, the one great truth:
Black rain on the temple roof."

- Dogen

"Nothing is left to you at this moment
but to have a good laugh."

- Zen Master

Contents

PART 5: AND THERE WAS A WORLD

Introduction

> "There are no steps to self-realisation."
>
> *- Nisargadatta Maharaj*

This book is about the utterly obvious. It's about the spiritual search, and the frustrations surrounding it. It's about the tendency of the mind to create and pursue goals. It's about those ultimate goals we set ourselves: *enlightenment, awakening, liberation, permanent happiness,* and how these goals can never really be reached, because – and here's the great discovery – the individual, the one who would reach any goals in the first place, has no more reality than a presently-arising belief. Which is to say, the individual does not really "exist" at all.

This book is about the *seeing-through* of this search for enlightenment, awakening, liberation and permanent happiness, the *seeing-through* of the individual, the *seeing-through* of the human drama in all its beauty and madness. And this seeing-through has nothing to do with a person, and nothing to do with time.

This book is not about picking up any new belief systems, or refining old ones. It's not about discovering any new path or method that will get you to some final destination. It's not about personal effort or lack of it, personal achievement or lack of it; it's not about self-improvement or self-knowledge; it's not about anything that anyone could ever teach you.

This book is about the utterly obvious. In fact, it's so utterly obvious, so painfully obvious, that no more words are really needed. No words can take you to where you already are: here and now. No words in any book could ever help the individual transcend himself.

But still, reading of this book may happen, and that's wonderful. And perhaps these little black squiggles may be of some use to a person looking for answers (but only because the words point back time and time again to the utterly obvious: this, this moment, is the answer of all answers ....)

Yes, this is really a book about nothing, but still, sometimes a book about nothing can be the most helpful thing, when the search for *something* has only ever led to frustration and bitter disappointment.

But to read these words with a goal in mind – that would be to miss the point entirely.

Now, I don't want to dwell on my past, because really it has nothing to do with this message, and very little to do with this present life. However, a little history may help to put this book into context.

Several years ago I embarked on a full-blown spiritual search, fuelled by the desire to escape the pain and misery of a lifetime.

I did not realise then that the desire to escape my pain and misery was the very thing that was giving life to it. In resisting the present appearance of what I felt to be suffering, that very suffering was being maintained and strengthened.

That which is resisted is given power. This seems to be a universal law.

It was the dissatisfaction with the present life which drove the spiritual search: a search for peace, for freedom, for an end to my miserable existence and all its problems, for an escape into a higher dimension, for liberation, for awakening, for enlightenment, for permanent happiness, permanent pleasure. The spiritual teachers and their beautifully worded books promised so much, and I wanted all of it!

Eventually, after months and months of meditation and self-enquiry, of questioning my thoughts and attempting to see through the ego, I finally came to believe that I was in the state spoken of by the spiritual masters as "enlightenment" or "liberation". I believed that enlightenment was a state which only a lucky few throughout the ages had ever reached, and that I, through my efforts, had finally done it.

However, what I didn't realise was that the belief that I was enlightened was just that: *another belief.* It never struck me that a truly enlightened person (and there is no such thing) would never for one moment claim to be enlightened, as the belief "*I am enlightened, others are not*" is just another way to separate human beings from each other, another act of violence, another way to maintain the very ego which was supposed to be ended in enlightenment.

The belief in personal enlightenment is just another way to maintain a strong sense of self: how very *un-enlightened!*

I came to see that "enlightenment" is not a state reserved for the lucky few, attained only by those who have been on the spiritual path for years, and who have carried out all the relevant practices and rituals, but it is something (and it is not really a "thing") available to all of us, all of the time, and so (and here's the secret) *no effort, or lack of it, is required.* Indeed, it is the very effort (or non-effort) to reach enlightenment which obscures the enlightenment that is always already present. It is our search for "something more" which apparently obscures the utterly obvious: the present moment, and everything that arises in it, is all there is. Don't believe this? Check – *it's always now.* Whatever happens, happens now. Is there ever a time when you cannot say "it is now"? Can anything happen if it is not happening now? Even memory (the story of a past) – is that not just a bundle of thoughts arising *presently*?

It's so obvious: what I was looking for all those years was not something that could ever be found, because it had never really been lost. Indeed, it is not really an "it" at all, not a thing amongst other things, but the very condition that allows the possibility of "things" in the first place.

Enlightenment is where we always already are, and in searching for it, we apparently lose it. Unfortunately, almost everything we do throughout our lives is part of this search, because almost everything we do implies that our salvation lies in the future, that peace and happiness and freedom are things that can be attained by us at some future time.

These days, the search for enlightenment, for a happiness outside the present happiness, for any sort of "self-improvement" whatsoever, has simply fallen away. And what is left? Is it still possible to live in this world when the desire for something beyond the ordinary has dissolved?

The message of this book is so simple, so obvious, so *present*, that the mind will never be able to grasp it. The message is nothing more or less than this: *There is nothing to "get"* ... and it is only the *idea* that there is something to get that makes it seem like there is something to get! And watch the mind as it tries to work all of this out, as it goes round in circles, comparing and contrasting this message with a billion other messages, as it keeps the search going in a billion different ways.

But here's the good news: this search only ever arises now as a belief, as thought. It doesn't need to be ended, because it's just another *harmless* present appearance. And anyway, the attempt to end the search would simply perpetuate the search ....

Simple and obvious – awakening is just this, here now. Just life, as it already is. And of course, this seems like a total paradox to a person hooked on self-improvement, to a mind trying to work it all out.

But there's nothing to work out, and there never was. The search is already over.

This book is about the utterly obvious, and nothing more.

Jeff Foster,
Oxford, UK

PART 1
A WALK IN THE RAIN

"In the gap between subject and object
lies the entire misery of humankind."
- J. Krishnamurti

As the story goes (and I can barely remember any of it now) I was walking through the rain on a cold autumn evening in Oxford. The sky was getting dark; I was wrapped up warm in my new coat. And suddenly and without warning, the search for *something more* apparently fell away, and with it all separation and loneliness.

And with the death of separation, I *was* everything that arose: I was the darkening sky, I was the middle-aged man walking his golden retriever, I was the little old lady hobbling along in her waterproofs. I was the ducks, the swans, the geese, the funny-looking bird with the red streak on its forehead. I was the trees in all their autumnal glory, I was the sludge sticking to my feet, I was my body, all of it, arms and legs and torso and face and hands and feet and neck and hair and genitals, the whole damn lot. I was the raindrops falling on my head (although it was not my head, I did not own it, but it was undeniably there, and so to call it "my head" is as good as anything). I was the *splish-splash* of water on the ground, I was the water collecting into puddles, I was the water swelling the pond until it looked fit to burst its banks, I was the trees soaked by water, I was my coat soaked by water, I was the water

1

soaking everything, I was everything being soaked, I was the water soaking itself.

And everything that for so long had seemed so ordinary had suddenly become so *extraordinary*, and I wondered if, in fact, it hadn't been this way all along: that perhaps for my whole life it had been this way, so utterly alive, so clear, so vibrant. Perhaps in my lifelong quest to reach the spectacular and the dramatic, I had missed the ordinary, and with it, and through it, and in it, the utterly extraordinary.

And the utterly extraordinary on this day was awash with rain, and I was not separate from any of it, that is to say, I was not there at all. As the old Zen master had said upon hearing the sound of the bell ringing, "There was no I, and no bell, just the ringing", so it was on this day: there was no "I" experiencing this clarity, there was only the clarity, only the utterly obvious presenting itself in each and every moment.

Of course, I had no way of knowing any of this at the time. At the time, thought was not there to claim any of this as an "experience". There was just what was happening, but no way of knowing it. The words came later.

And there was an all-pervading feeling that everything was *okay* with the world, there was an equanimity and a sense of peace which seemed to underlie everything there was; it was as though everything was simply a manifestation of this peace, as if nothing existed apart from peace, in its infinite guises. And I was the peace, and the duck over there was it too, and the wrinkly old lady still waddling along was the peace, and the peace was all around, everything just vibrated with it, this grace, this presence that was utterly unconditional and free, this overwhelming love that seemed to be the very essence of the world, the very reason for it, the Alpha and the Omega of it all. The word "God" seemed to point to it too, and the word "Tao", and "Buddha". This was the self-authenticating experience that all religions seemed to point to in the end. This seemed to be the very essence of faith: death of the self, death of the "little me" with its petty desires and complaints and futile plans, death of everything that separates the individual from God, death of even the idea of God himself (*"If you see the Buddha, kill him"*) and a plunge into Nothingness, the Nothingness that reveals itself as the God beyond God, the Nothingness that all things are in their essence, the Nothingness that gives rise to all form, the Nothingness that is the world itself in all its pain and wonder, the Nothingness that is total Fullness.

And yet this so-called "religious experience" is not really an experience at all, since the one who experiences, the "me", is the very thing which is no more. No, this is something beyond, something prior to, all experience. It is the foundation of all experience, the ground of existence itself, and nobody could ever experience that, even if the world lasted another billion years.

That day, there was nobody there, and yet everything was there in its place. Beyond experience or lack of it, there were the ducks flapping their little wings, there were the raindrops trickling down my neck, there were the puddles under my shoes which were now caked in mud, there was the grey sky, there were other bodies, just like mine, splashing through the puddles, some walking their dogs, some alone, some cuddling up to their loved ones, some running frantically to escape the downpour.

And there was a great compassion. Not a sentimental compassion, not a narcissistic compassion, but a compassion that seemed to be part of what it meant to be alive on that day, a compassion which seemed to be the very essence of life, a compassion which seemed to pulsate through all living things, a compassion which said that none of us were separate from each other, that nothing at all was really separate from anything else, that your pain was identical to my pain, that your joy was my joy, not because these were principles we'd read in the Bible or taken on authority from those we held in high esteem, not because these were ideals that we tried to live up to, but because this seemed to be the way of things, this seemed to be the nature of manifestation: that we were all expressions of something infinitely larger than ourselves.

But even the word "ourselves" seemed to imply that we were separate, and therefore this was a compassion which was beyond words, beyond language; indeed this compassion transcended any idea of "compassion", this compassion arose from the fact that *there actually is no separation at all*, that separation is an illusion, that in fact we *are* each other, that I am you, that you are me, that we cannot be ourselves without others, that I cannot be I without you, and you cannot be you without me, not in some wishy-washy lovey-dovey sentimental way, but really, honestly: we need each other, we are bound to each other, we cannot live without each other, we cannot live without everything else. I cannot live without that tree I'm walking under, without the raindrops that have made their way down my back, without the old woman who's managed to waddle a little further down the path (she's being so very careful to avoid the puddles), without the pond, without the ducks, without the swans, without my new coat keeping me warm, without the man with the dog who smiles and says "Hi" as he walks past.

We are bound to each other, all things are bound to all things, which is to say there are not really any separate "things" at all, there is only Oneness, only the whole, only the Buddha, only Christ, only the Tao, only God Himself, and nothing exists apart from anything else.

And so to say that on that day there was no "I" is really to say that there was only God, there was only Christ, there was only the Tao, only Buddha, only Oneness, only Spirit, and Jeff had exploded into it all, Jeff was nowhere to be found, in the sense that he was not separate from everything that arose. Jeff was just a story spun by a storyteller with a vivid imagination, Jeff was missing from the scene and yet infused into it, Jeff was nothing and he was everything, he was present to his own absence and absent to his presence, he was life itself, in its entirety, and yet he, in all truth, had died.

And yes, there were tears. What else is there to do but cry at such a discovery? A discovery which really wasn't a discovery at all, because nothing had been found, since nothing had really ever been lost. This clarity had always been there, I'd just been looking elsewhere my whole life and ignoring the utterly obvious. God had always been right there, in the present moment, in the midst of things, but I'd spent my life seeking Him in the future. The Buddha Mind had been my own mind, always, but I'd spent years trying to attain it. Christ had been crucified and resurrected and was walking in the midst of us, drenching our lives in unconditional love, but for a lifetime I had assumed he was *elsewhere*, in some other world (or in this world but not in my own life, at least).

No, nothing had been found, because nothing had ever been lost. But perhaps it was the realisation of the utterly obvious that hit me that day, the realisation that there was *nothing to realise*, that everything I ever wanted was always right there in front of me and always would be, that peace and love and joy were always freely available in each and every moment, that love, pure unconditional love, the love of Jesus, the love of Buddha, the love that passes all understanding was the very ground of all things, the very reason for anything being here in the first place. It was there, always there, always waiting patiently for me to return home.

And there, in the rain, on that day, I knew finally that I was home, and what's more, that I would always be home, that I *had always* been home, through it all, through all the tears and the pain, through the dark times and the desperate times and all the times I thought I'd never make it, through all those times and more, the Home of all Homes had been there. The possibility of the Kingdom of Heaven was always present, the grace of

God was always an open invitation, through thick and thin, through sickness and through health, through all that, world without end ....

And there were other times like this, when Jeff melted away and with him all separation and isolation; there were times when tears flowed at the awesomeness of this thing we call life, at the fact that there are "things" at all; there were times when there was a love so fierce that the heart was fit to burst, and there were times when there was simply nothing, no existence, no world, no God, nothing, no-thing.

And these times were attached to and given importance. They were labelled "spiritual experiences" or "awakenings" and there was a great excitement.

These days, all that nonsense has faded away. There is just the living of a very ordinary life. Whether "Jeff" is there or not is of no importance. But through it all, there is a sense of equanimity, an "okayness" with everything that arises, a deep, unshakeable certainty that everything is happening exactly as it should, and this includes the pain as well as the pleasure, the anger as well as the joy.

Perhaps what has been seen is this: whatever we take ourselves to be, whatever character we have been assigned in the great play of life, this character arises out of something infinitely larger than itself. This character cannot sustain itself by itself: it has no foundations (as the great existentialist philosophers have seen). No, a greater power is at work, an infinitely greater power. Call it God, call it the Tao, call it by a thousand different names, it is That which gives rise to all things, it is That without which there are no things at all. It is not something that can be reached through thinking, as it gives rise to thinking. It is not something that can be found at the end of a long search, for it is that which allows seeking in the first place. In fact, it is not something that can be spoken of, as it is that in which speech arises.

And what is it?

It is this moment, and everything that happens in it.

This moment is the only place where all things arise, indeed nothing can arise if it does not arise now. Any idea of yourself, if it arises, must arise now.

All sounds are present sounds, all feelings are present feelings, all thoughts are present thoughts.

This will never be captured in words, and yet we spend our lives trying to do precisely that. In this moment, you (what you take yourself to be) only exist as thought. Which is to say that right now, in this moment, "you" do not exist at all. This is exactly what was seen (by nobody) on that rainy day: the individual is only an apparent individual, the individual is just a body of thought, arising in the present moment. The individual does not "exist" as this tree exists, or this flower exists. It could never have that solidity, that certainty, that definite shape and form. We are without foundation, we swim in a sea of nothingness. As Sartre would say, we are always fleeing ourselves, always grasping desperately at what we call "self" but ending up with a handful of nothing.

And this gives rise to great anxiety, because somewhere, deep down, we know that we are simply castles in the air, that we have no greater reality than that. And so we try desperately to build foundations, to grow roots, to anchor ourselves, and we cling to things, we attach ourselves to jobs, to other people, to ideas and ideals and ideologies, hoping desperately that these things will save us, that they will provide the foundation that we lack in ourselves. We cling to beliefs, to idols, to man-made gods and religions, but all beliefs exist in the shadow of doubt, and this can only ever give rise to more anxiety, because underneath it all, we are terrified that what we cling to will dissolve. As the Buddhists have always said, all forms are impermanent. And so we cling more tightly. And the vicious circle goes on, round and round, until death.

But what was seen on that autumn day cuts through all of these feeble attempts to anchor ourselves. What was seen is the secret that is not really a secret at all. What was seen is the utterly obvious: we are always already anchored in something far beyond ourselves. We are always already anchored in the present moment, in the God beyond God, in the divine. And yet virtually everything we do in this life implies that we are not. Everything we do to become more present, everything we do to get closer to God – these are the very things that magnify our alienation from the Source. The secret is that what we are so desperately seeking throughout our lives is *always* right in front of us. The divine is *already* present in the utterly ordinary things of life.

God is always with us. And that is not something that we can "achieve"; it is something that already is. Indeed, it is the essence of life itself.

It was a very ordinary walk on a very ordinary, and very wet, autumn day. And yet, in that ordinariness, the extraordinary revealed itself, shining through the wetness and the darkness and the sludge on the ground, shining so brightly that I was no more, that I dissolved into that brightness and became it.

And yet, that makes it sound way too special. That day, in the rain, nothing really happened at all. It was just a very ordinary walk on a very ordinary day.

I left through the large iron gates, crossed the road and waited for the bus, huddling in the shelter with several others.

Nothing had changed and everything had changed. I had glimpsed something, something deep and profound and in some ways shocking, and yet something that was utterly ordinary and somewhat unsurprising. Yes, it was *unsurprising* that the very ordinary should turn out to be the only meaning of life, that who I took myself to be should turn out to be just a nice fairy story.

Yes, it was unsurprising, that the divine should be in the utterly ordinary, that God should be one with the world, present in and as each and every thing.

I boarded the bus and as the rain streamed down the dirty windows I smiled to myself. What a gift – to be alive now of all moments, to be in this body of all bodies, to be here, in this place of all places, even though it is all a dream, even though it is all impermanent, even though if we really look, we find nothing but emptiness. But still, out of infinite possibilities, you are here, and it is now. It didn't have to be this way, but it is. It won't be this way forever, but it is now.

This is not the story of "Jeff's awakening" although undoubtedly that story will arise. Yes, the story "Jeff is awakened" is a good story: it sets up "awakening" as something to get. Something that you want, something that can be found, given time, something that some individuals have apparently "attained". What a load of bullshit! There is only ever *this*, what is presently arising, and no fictional character (and this includes any so-called "awakened" fictional character) could ever be anything other than a good story, arising now.

This is the only miracle: that you are here (whoever or whatever you are) and it is now. It doesn't take a walk in the rain to see this, not at all. In fact there are no requirements whatsoever. You don't need to be anyone or anywhere else. You can start from exactly where you are. Indeed, that's the only place you ever start. Here and now.

And yet, "you" cannot start at all. There is no path that could ever take you to where you already are, and even if there was, the person who would follow that path has no more reality than a presently arising story.

PART 2
REFLECTIONS

"We eat, excrete, sleep, and get up;
This is our world.
All we have to do after that... is to die."
- Ikkyu

Just a Thought

This has nothing to do with effort. This has nothing to do with understanding.

Nothing to do with process, nothing to do with praxis.

Nothing to do with lack of process or praxis.

This is not about seeing anything new, or getting rid of anything old.

This is not something the mind could ever grasp. Nor does the mind need to give up its grasping.

This is nothing personal, nor does it have anything to do with the "impersonal".

This is not about choiceless awareness, or seeing through the ego, or self-enquiry.

This cannot be expressed using concepts. Nor will it ever be expressed in the absence of concepts.

This is not about words. Not even these words.

This is not about getting anywhere.

This has nothing to do with any kind of future achievement.

This is not about following a path: there is no path, although there may be the idea of "a path".

This is not about reaching a higher state: there are no higher states, although there may be concepts about "higher states".

This is not about becoming anything, although beliefs about that may arise too.

This is certainly not about "putting an end to the I". Only an "I" would want that.

This is most definitely not about "becoming more present" - the present was never lost in the first place.

This is not about waiting for an event called liberation – that would require time, and a "me" who would eventually become liberated.

This has nothing to do with going "beyond" anything – there is nothing to go beyond, and nobody who could go beyond even if they wanted to.

This is not about enlightenment. There is no such thing as enlightenment.

This is not about awakening. There is no such thing as awakening.

This is not about enlightened individuals passing on their understanding. That's a good story, and a compelling one, but it's just a story, and has no deeper reality.

This is not something that could be of any use to anyone.

This is not something that anyone would ever want.

But no matter – the "me" who would want this is just a thought anyway.

Just a thought.

This is It!

And so, after years of seeking in a billion different ways, we are only ever left with the present moment, which is *this* moment. Not the idea "the present moment", but quite literally, *this*, the present appearance of it all, beyond all words and concepts.

The beating of the heart (thud, thud, thud!)

Breathing. In, out. In, out ...

The roar of traffic outside.

The feeling of this book in your hands.

Thoughts arising, dissolving, arising ...

No matter what we've been through, no matter what we've "discovered", no matter what we've "realised", it's always here, and it's always now, and the individual (that is, "you") who went through all that stuff, who "discovered" and "realised" and did a thousand different things in the name of finding himself, was only ever a thought, a story, a belief.

Right now, "you" are quite literally a fiction. That is not to deny the fiction: the fiction arises, as it always has. Let it be.

Perhaps liberation, if anything, is the seeing-through of this fiction. That is, the recognition, by no-one, of the fiction as a fiction.

And yet, even that is saying too much. Even that little string of words sets "liberation" up as something to get, something to achieve. Oh, the mind loves that story: *"If I could just see the fiction as a fiction, I would be in liberation!"* And the search for liberation goes on, and the mind has saved itself once again.

Liberation is not something that an individual can get, like he can get a nice suntan, or a bigger bank balance, or a shiny new sports car. It's not something a person can achieve like he can achieve a high score in an IQ test. It's not something that can be reached through effort, or persistence, or luck, or anything else.

Liberation is not about words and concepts. However, we have to use words (it's hard not to when you're writing a book!), and therefore we inevitably fall into the trap of seeing liberation as a goal, as something to look forward to in the future, as some sort of ideal.

But the message of this book is that liberation, if anything, is the seeing-through of this very seeking. Liberation, if anything, is the seeing-through of the search for liberation, of the search for something more meaningful than what is already the case, of the search for something other than this, this present appearance.

But don't we spend our lives searching for something other than this? And so liberation, if it is anything, is the seeing-through of the *entire* human drama, of every-thing, quite literally everything that makes up our lives.

For the character "Jeff", everything has changed and yet nothing has changed at all. Perhaps the only difference is that these days, "Jeff" is simply recognised as a character, a story floating about in awareness. He has no deeper reality than that.

Liberation is so utterly simple, so utterly obvious. The search is already over, and what we were always seek-ing is nothing more than this present appearance: just this, right here, right now. There is nothing more. There never was.

The End of Spirituality

"Love has befriended Hafiz so completely.
It has turned to ash and freed me
Of every concept and image my mind has ever known."
- Hafiz

After months and months of intensive questioning, meditation and other so-called "self-realisation" practices (as taught by Ramana Maharshi, J Krishnamurti, Nisargadatta Maharaj, to name but a few), I came to believe that I had seen through the "I" once and for all. There were mind-blowing spiritual experiences, there was a sense of deep peace, there were long periods without thought, there were tears at the most ordinary of things (chairs, tables, trees, cats...).

I came to believe that I was enlightened, and that others were not, although at the time I did not see this as a *belief* at all, because I believed it to be true, and therefore not a belief. But that was just another belief!

I came to believe that I was somehow *special*.

However, this belief could not hold itself up. No belief can.

And so after a while, I saw through this idea of exclusive personal enlightenment, and I came to believe that in fact everyone was enlightened ... except that some people just hadn't "realised" it yet. I came to believe that it was somehow my duty to let other people in on the secret, in order to bring an end to their suffering.

However, the mind wouldn't let me get away with that either. I soon began to realise that nobody could ever become "enlightened" in the first place – that would just be another belief, and wasn't enlightenment supposed to be the seeing-through of all beliefs?

And yet, even *that* was just another belief.

I realised that *everything* was just a thought, just a belief, just mind! How could we ever know anything? And if we couldn't, how could we ever know that?

If I was enlightened, how would I ever know it? These people who claimed to have reached "liberation" or "seen through all beliefs", how could they ever know? On what basis could they make their assertions? "Enlightenment" and "liberation" – weren't those just more words, more beliefs, more concepts?

I could not get around this. I was going round in circles. It was all just belief! No matter what I thought had been "seen", or "realised", or "understood", by somebody or by nobody (yes, I had picked up the language of non-duality), this was just more thought, more separation, more language, more of the search. It was a vicious, violent circle, and there was no escape.

There was a great frustration and exhaustion, and a

deep, dark despair at the ridiculous nature of the whole damn stupid spiritual search.

And the midst of that despair, something gave way.

These days, all seeking has apparently died. I have no idea how or why, but it seems to be the case.

This is not something I have achieved... not at all, not at all!

And so ...

... what is left?

Breathing.

Heart beating.

Sensations in the body.

A tuna salad.

The crunch of the lettuce leaves.

The faint fishy smell of the tuna.

The fork coming up ... up ... up ... CRUNCH!

❀ Owned by no-one, understood by no-one. Just this. ❀

Awash in nothingness, bathed in emptiness, and yet totally full, full as full can be. And beyond all these words, beyond any thought anyone has ever had, there is that fork coming up again, undeniably so ... here it comes! ... and the teeth chomping down ... CRUNCH!

This CRUNCH! is the end of all spirituality.

Before enlightenment, crunch tuna salad.

After enlightenment, crunch tuna salad.

And of course, there is no before or after at all, and certainly no enlightenment. That's just a good story.

The Seeking Game

The spiritual search can only ever end in frustration, because what is sought is identical with that which is doing the seeking. We seek an end to the search, ignoring the blindingly obvious: the seeking implies that there is, in fact, something to be found. In fact, the entire search rests on that assumption.

That assumption, indeed, is the search itself. Is it really surprising that this search could go on for an entire lifetime?

And with the search comes identification as "the one who seeks". Seeking implies a seeker. But in seeking the end of the seeker, the seeker is once again ignoring the utterly, utterly obvious: it's the seeking that's the "problem", in the sense that the seeking implies there is something wrong with now. The seeking implies a resistance to what is, a resistance which is identical to the self, to "me".

The seeking implies a future, a future where the seeker will be no more. And this future seeker-free existence is sought desperately. But as long as there is seeking, there will be a "me" who is seeking, which is exactly the thing that the seeking was supposed to put an end to. But the one who seeks, and the one who is supposed to do any sort of "seeing through", is present right now, in this moment, as thought, and indeed that's the only reality any person has. And even if it was possible to reach "liberation", if it cannot be done now, it cannot be done at all.

This is all there is, and a future is not required to "see through" this or "realise" this. In fact, it is the search itself that implies that this is not all there is, that there is something more. The search itself is a denial of the utterly obvious and utterly simple presence which is identical with this moment.

And yet we carry on seeking, hoping that one day we'll become like those enlightened guys, the ones who talk endlessly about peace and love and joy and the end of suffering, and offer a path which you can follow.

But peace and love and joy are right here, right now.

And peace and love and joy are so simple.

And this is what they look like:

The heart beating.

The tap dripping.

The washing machine whirring.

Breathing.

Thoughts floating through.

Hunger.

Pain in the chest, a tenderness in the stomach.

The television buzzing.

This is the miracle we've been seeking our whole lives. It was always staring us in the face.

The Message of Nonduality

The message of nonduality is simple: nothing is separate from anything else. But apparent separation is at the root of everything the individual does; indeed, the individual is nothing *but* apparent separation, and that separation drives the entire spiritual search and the quest for the dissolution of the ego, as well as all worldly pursuits.

But the seeking mind (that is, "you", the individual) will never be able to grasp this message, as, to the mind, this message is nothing but its own dissolution, that is, its own death.

Yes, this message is death, but it is also life. All life is here, all life is now, and the mind cannot accept that, because the mind is nothing more than a denial of life. The mind cannot grasp the totality, so it creates a world, a little world of knowledge and values and meaning. And that's fine, but the intellect will never grasp the vastness of life, because life, that is, this, is prior to intellect; indeed, the intellect already arises out of the totality, out of this.

In this moment, all the problems of an individual are merely thoughts, and since thoughts already simply appear in the play of life, thought is already impersonal, already liberated, because consciousness already transcends, *inherently* transcends, everything that appears in it.

But this is already getting way too heady, too intellectual. The reality is simple, obvious, present. Thoughts appear now: they are not "my" thoughts, they are just thoughts. They are not "my" problems, they are just problems. This is not "my" life, this is just life.

Life plays out, and I am both utterly immersed in it, and utterly absent. And these are not polar opposites: to be immersed fully, is to be fully absent.

Fully immersed, fully absent. And yet there is still the noise of traffic outside, still the *click-click* of the boiler switching on and off, still the sound of breathing, still the *tap-tap* of the rain at the windows, still the tiredness in the body, still the sensations, moment by precious moment ....

And so, even though I am fully absent, life carries on.

Even though I am nowhere to be found, life cannot, will not cease, not now, not ever.

Contradictions

*T*his is it, but it appears as though it's not. There is no individual, but it appears as though there is.

Nobody is typing these words, but these words appear to have been typed.

There is nothing, no-thing. And yet, there is undeniably something going on.

Contradiction city!

And the poor little mind struggles with all of this, trying to make sense of it, trying to understand, trying to realise, trying to "get it" at last.

But there is no way to go beyond these apparent contradictions, because the attempt to go beyond the contradictions actually just maintains the contradictions, strengthens the contradictions.

And the attempt to go beyond the contradictions fuels the sense of "I" (*the one who is attempting to go beyond the contradictions*).

There may be the idea that once the contradictions are "overcome", there will be some sort of enlightenment experience, some sort of awakening, some sort of peace.

In other words, there may be the belief that there is something to "get" by overcoming the contradictions.

And there are many (undoubtedly well-meaning) spiritual teachers all over the world who help to fuel this search. Many teachers make claims such as: "I am enlightened! Follow me and you can be like this too!"

But this search only maintains and strengthens the sense of "me" as a "seeker".

Which is fine, really.

But perhaps there will come a time, and paradoxically that time is now, when the search is seen through. And then the utterly, utterly obvious reveals itself:

This is it!

This moment!

The search is already over. You are already that which you seek. You always were.

The search was always in vain; it only ever brought you back to here, to now, reading these words. The search always implied that this – this moment - wasn't enough.

But how could this not be enough? This is all there is! Don't believe me? Just look around. *This is this. This is here. This is now. This is utterly undeniable.*

Vicious Circles

The "I"
who wants to be free from the "I"
maintains and strengthens the very "I"
he seeks to free himself from.

The individual
who claims he is liberated from individuality
is more of an individual than ever.

The person who claims to be enlightened
and free from desire
is still not free from the desire
to go on about
his so-called "enlightenment".

The self
who claims to have seen through the self
is still only a self:
a self claiming to have seen through the self!

Only a self would claim to be free from self.

Only an individual would claim to be free from
individuality.

Only someone entrenched in their beliefs would proclaim
their freedom from all belief.

This is not to condemn anyone.

And no doubt the character "Jeff" has at times been guilty of some or all of these things.

But now, I would ask, with respect,

WHO gets enlightened?
WHO sees through the self?
WHO is liberated?
WHO is awakened?
WHO transcends beliefs?
WHO sees through illusion?
WHO "gets" this?

You see, this message has nothing to do with personal achievement.

If anything, it has everything to do with personal failure. Total failure, utter disappointment.

And in that total failure of the self, something else may shine through. But it's nothing to do with a "somebody" becoming "enlightened". If anything, it's that very idea that is seen through, by no-one.

And how could that ever, ever, be a personal achievement?

A Deadly Message

Who can stand this message? This message points to nothing less than the destruction of the seeker, the annihilation of the one who wants answers.

This message is death. And who really wants to die?

That's why this message is rejected so often. Nobody wants to hear that everything they think they are, all their hopes and dreams and ambitions and achievements, all their so-called past experiences, all their plans for the future, all their relationships, everything they take to be part of their "life" is nothing but an illusion, a story, a play, a game, a dance of awareness, playing out now. Everything they are is nothing but thought. And perhaps not even that.

And who would want to hear that?

You cannot hear this message. You cannot understand it. You cannot "get" it.

The mind cannot annihilate itself. The mind cannot see past itself. All attempts to "get" this message are nothing but the mind trying to "get" the end of itself.

Do you really want to die? Of course you don't. Everything you take to be yourself is nothing but a fight against death, a fight against impermanence, a seeking for something more than is obviously, simply, presently the case. What you take to be "you" gives some idea of permanence, gives some sort of feeling of a life story extended from the past into the future, gives comfort in a seemingly terrifying world.

But what reality does any of that have? "My life story" is a story arising now. "My past and my future" are thoughts arising now. What you take to be yourself has no more reality than that. That is why we can say that this life is simply a play of appearances. There is an apparent individual, but on closer inspection, there's simply nothing there.

Still, let's not deny appearances. Only an appearance would deny appearances anyway...

Yes, this message is death, but in that death there is also life. Life was never separate from death in the first place.

All of this can sound very heady, very conceptual. But what these words try (and fail miserably) to point to is so utterly obvious: It's just this. Really, I mean it. Just this.

Right now, everything you take yourself to be has already faded into memory. In a sense, you are already dead. And yet, there is apparent life. Life and death: no difference, truly.

The End of Suffering

This is the end of suffering, because it is the end of an "I" who suffers.

That is not to say that suffering cannot still happen, but that if it happens, it happens for no-one, and therefore it cannot really be called "suffering" at all, because only a *someone* would put a name to suffering, and in that naming, create it.

We create the very suffering we seek to be rid of. This is not a new message: the Buddha spoke clearly about it, thousands of years ago.

But saying that we create our own suffering implies that, having somehow "realised" this, we can put an end to our suffering, through effort. No, this very idea is responsible for the suffering in the first place.

Is there suffering if suffering is not known as suffering? Is there suffering if there is not someone there who wants to be free from suffering?

Is there any suffering at all apart from the desire to be free from suffering?

All there is, is this, this present appearance.

And in this present appearance, there may be physical pain.

But physical pain is simply not a problem. Not until "I" come in, and call it "pain", that is. And with that labelling comes the implication that the present experience is unpleasant and must be escaped.

And there's the suffering, right there. Resistance is suffering. And yet resisting the resistance (the aim of most so-called spiritual practices) simply adds to the problem, feeds the problem.

No, the way out of suffering is not through resistance. Nor is it through acceptance.

Both resistance and acceptance require a person separate from their suffering, and at this moment, a person separate from suffering is just a story.

No, the way out of suffering is not through any movement in relation to suffering. Any movement in relation to suffering maintains suffering as suffering. Any movement in relation to suffering perpetuates the very disease we are trying to cure.

The way out of suffering is through death: death of the one who suffers.

Not physical death, no, that's too easy. It's one way, yes, but it's too easy.

The way out of suffering is through a death more radical than any physical death. Physical death is in time, and the way out of suffering cannot be in time, as it is time which has created suffering in the first place ("Soon, I'll be free from suffering...").

The way out of suffering is through suffering itself.

Remember Jesus on the cross.

Right now, *who* is suffering?

Who is the one who is upset at the present situation?

Who is the one who wants to be free from their present problems?

These days, when I look to find the answers to these questions, when I look to see if there is anyone there who suffers, anyone who could be free from their suffering, I find nothing but the looking, which is to say, I "find" nothing at all.

"The life I am trying to grasp is the me that is trying to grasp it."

Yes, and the suffering I am trying to flee is the me that is trying to flee it.

The Myth of Choice

"I am a person who can choose" – the root of all confusion!

No, there was never any choice in the first place. "I choose" is a good story, spun by a storyteller who creates himself in choosing himself.

In reality, what happens, happens. The story of choice is simply part of what happens.

Why did it take a whole lifetime to see this?

No matter. "A whole lifetime" is another story, arising now.

What a relief, to be free from choice. Whatever happens, happens. Whatever will happen, will happen. Whatever has happened, couldn't have happened any other way. "It could have happened differently"– another story, another illusion. The root of all suffering.

No choice, and yet life happens, and there are undoubtedly apparent choices made. But really, "we" have no control at all.

This is why many spiritual teachings talk about surrender to life, to God, to the Unknown. In surrender, personal choice collapses, and there is relief from the burden of volition.

But remember: "you" cannot surrender, and choosing not to choose would just be another choice.

Beyond choice, or lack of it, there is simply this: what is present happening. I can apparently choose to go and make a cup of tea, but it's only an apparent choice: where did the idea to make a cup of tea come from? Did the idea just "pop into my head"? And who is responsible for that "popping"?

How wonderful: life plays out, presently, and everything happens exactly as it should, when it should. What freedom in that!

The idea of choice is the root of all violence, separation, narcissism, and therefore suffering. The idea of choice implies that there is an individual who is separate from life, who somehow creates his own life in choosing it. What violence! How could I ever separate myself from this? Who am I, to claim that I have power over this? How egotistical, to think that I can make a difference!

And yet, and yet, for all of that, how wonderful, how exciting, to believe in choice, to believe that I am an individual who can change the world, who can make things happen, for myself and for others!

So let's not deny apparent choice! It can be fun, to apparently choose to go to the cinema, to apparently choose to read a certain book or go for a walk in the park. The world is nothing but a play of apparent choices!

Did you choose to read these words? Or is reading simply happening?

Yes, the thought "I chose to read this book" may arise. But to *whom* does this thought arise?

Can you choose to think or not think about this?

The Elephant

"What should I do with my life?"

Ah, this question can never be answered, for the "you" that is trying to work it all out, is the very life that is being thought about.

Here's what to do with your life: *do what you do.* That is all.

That is to say, whatever happens, happens. See, it's already happening: now, now and now. Life is only a problem when the questions begin:

"Should I be doing something else?"
"Have I made the right decisions?"
"What will become of me?"

These questions arise now. There is the idea that once the questions are answered, there will be freedom from confusion.

But do we really have any choice in the matter? Can we think our way out of confusion?

Try this experiment: don't think of an elephant. Whatever you do, don't think of an elephant.

Can you choose not to think of an elephant?

Go on, try really hard. Choose not to think of an elephant.

See, there's no real choice, is there?

If you can't even choose not to think of an elephant, you don't have much chance in choosing the big stuff, do you?

Whatever happens, happens. And then "I" come in, and don't want what happens to happen.

Hopeless!

And I can claim that I had total control over what happened, or I can claim I had no control, and was just a victim of fate.

Between these two opposites the entire human drama plays out.

PART 3
DIALOGUE

"There's nothing equal to wearing clothes and eating food.
Outside this there are neither Buddhas nor Patriarchs."
- Zenrin Kushû

Open Discussion
15th February 2007, Sutton Coldfield, UK

Jeff: So, there's a search for something *more*. And we don't quite know what it is that we're searching for, but we do know that this, this present life, is a problem. And the search *implies* that problem, doesn't it? If this present life was fine, why would we search? And the message of nonduality is this: the search for Oneness, liberation, God, perfect peace, perfect happiness – and it goes under a billion different names – is just an attempt to escape what is presently happening. And this "me", this seeker, the one who wants to be free, the one who wants to reach liberation or Oneness, this "me" already simply arises *in* liberation, *in* Oneness.

In other words, there's an idea of "me" now, isn't there? There's an idea arising presently of me and my life, isn't there? And the message is this: *already* the individual is just that: something arising presently, a story, a belief. Who you are is just a story! Just a story being told now. And there's nobody telling that story – that's the illusion! *There's no "me" telling the story of "me" – there's just the story of "me".*

But then we read our spiritual books, and we hear that in order to achieve enlightenment we have to end the "me". That's a common one, isn't it? That we have to put an end to the "me". But who would want to put an end to "me" but a "me"? And then you go round in circles and it becomes very frustrating, to try and end "me"! In the story of "Jeff", that's what happened for years. Round and round in circles of thought, trying to put an end to "me and my problems"! Me trying to end myself!

And some of us get attracted to nonduality teachings, and we go to meetings to see people who have apparently ended the "me", who have ended the search. And these people tell us there's no such thing as awakening or liberation! And yet the search goes on! We can't accept that there's nothing more than this. How can we accept that?

Q: But haven't some people who have searched found what they were looking for? Aren't there some people who just get there, who just arrive at Oneness? You're making it all seem so complicated ...

You're right, I am. That's all words can do, complicate. The very fact that I'm talking implies that I have something to say, that there's something worth hearing, that there may be something to get! That perhaps I've discovered something, reached some sort of understanding and am giving a "talk" on it. But if that story is happening ("Jeff has something to teach") then that's just a story. The story that fuels the search! And you're right, there's the story that there are people who, as you say, have reached some sort of "higher state", some state that is better than "your" state. "I want their state – this state isn't enough!" And that search goes on in a billion different ways, for a lifetime.

For a lifetime, we're searching, and what do we really want? What do we really want but an end to that search! Because that search is the problem, that search implies that there's something wrong with this. This message is so simple!

And the only reason this apparent character "Jeff" is sitting here giving this talk is that at some point (and I don't really like to say "at some point" because it sounds like something definite happened, something concrete) there was a *seeing through* of this futile search for something more.

And some may ask "If the search is the problem, how do I end it? I've been trying to end it for many years, but it still goes on! Help!" But what we don't see is that the desire to end the search is more of the same! The search to end the search is more searching!

And the search only ever brought us here! An entire lifetime of seeking in a billion different ways, trying to improve ourselves, trying to become something else, only served to bring us here, to hear this message that there was never anything to get in the first place!

Q. So you're saying we should surrender?

But isn't that what the search is, the attempt to surrender? To ease the burden of "me"? We would if we could!

If only it was that easy! But it's obviously not, because then everybody would just surrender.

We read these spiritual books and hear about "enlightened people", people who have ended the search, people who are completely content with the present moment, people who don't desire anything, who never have any problems. And then we look at ourselves, and compared to them, we're just miseries! And there's the search right there!

Q. So for you, the desire to change things has gone away? And that is liberation?

It's that very story – that there is a possibility of liberation – that perpetuates the search for liberation. There is no liberation, there is just this. And paradoxically, this *is* the liberation that is sought.

Q. So there is no freedom from this?

Doesn't the idea that there is a freedom outside of this perpetuate the search? The idea that there's a freedom that I can get, and it's out there, and it's in the future? And that makes *this* into a problem.

Q. So if there's a sense of boredom here, then that's what's arising …

Yes, and it's only a problem if "you" want to be free from it.

Q. Yes, but there's a suggestion in the literature that some people have somehow found a place of ease.

Yes, there is that story. And in the story of my life, I devoured the literature. And I did the meditation and self-enquiry, and I had mind-blowing spiritual experiences, and so on. But it's all just a story! It's the story of "Jeff", arising now. A story being told now. That's the only reality we have! Just a story! And there are different stories being told. Just Oneness, and stories arising, and those stories are as much an expression of Oneness as anything else.

Q. But the sages have had a consistent story: when the self is seen through, an ease will appear.

But who would see through the self? Only a self would claim to have seen through the self.

There's a story that "I can put an end to myself", isn't there? There's the story of individuals who have ended individuality, that there are people out there who have ended their sense of self.

Q. They are at one with themselves?

Yes, that's the *story*. And that's a story arising now.

Q. That's your story as well, isn't it?

That's a story I could tell.

Q. It doesn't have any significance?

No, no significance.

Q. What do you mean by "story"?

A concept, a belief, a thought. So, there's this! *(bangs on table)*. And there's a story about this apparent "Jeff", his life, his past. And that's it. That's the only reality I have, that's the only reality any of us have.

Undeniably, there's this *(bangs again on table!)*. The heart beating. Breathing. There's a clock ticking. Sighing. Thoughts might be happening …

Q. You've said….

Questions happening! *(laughter)*

Q. You've said that you once thought you were enlightened. What's changed?

How would anybody *know* that they were enlightened? It's a story! "I'm enlightened" is a story! Because there's only this! This, this present appearance of everything! And then the story "I'm enlightened" happens. And it's so insignificant! A while back, I thought I'd discovered something wonderful. But that's all faded away now. That's just another way to separate: "I'm enlightened, you're not! I've ended the search, you haven't!" And there's a violence there, a separation. If anything, what's been seen is exactly that.

Q. So … who are you?

That question doesn't mean anything. Of course, if I was asked, I'd reply "I'm Jeff". But it has no deeper reality than a story being told now. But that story drives us mad, doesn't it? Because that "me" could always be improved! I could be happier, I could have a bigger bank balance, I could find a more loving partner. And there's always that sense of incompleteness, of striving. But that story of me, "me and my difficult life, me and my problems", it's *just* a story, and stories can't hurt you.

But it's never seen as a story. And there's a real seriousness that comes with that, a sense of having to defend oneself, maintain oneself, improve oneself. And that's all fine, I'm not denying any of it! In the story there can be some wonderful experiences. You can get married, you can have kids, it can be wonderful. But whatever has happened in your life, it has no deeper reality than a story being told now. The past has no deeper reality than a story being told now! It's memory.

And so, who am I? I could tell the story. But I *am* that story! The illusion is that there is a separate "me" telling the story. That there's a little "me" inside telling the story. No – there's just the story. And there's the sound of the clock ticking. And there's some voices, out there. Some rustling of feet. Thoughts happening, maybe. And this is it! This is life. This moment. Not the concept "this moment", but *this*! And this is not a problem, until the search happens, because the search says "this isn't enough, I want more, I want something else! I want enlightenment! When I'm enlightened, this will be different!"

Q. Is suffering an identification with the thought story?

What is suffering apart from the search? The search to escape what is presently happening? For example, if there is physical pain, it's simply not a problem until "I" want to be free from it. The pain is not a problem, until the search begins! And I am that search! The "me" who wants to be free from pain is the problem. And beyond all concepts of "pain", there is this, this burning sensation in the leg, undeniably so, happening, happening, now, now, now! *(Slaps leg).* And it's not a problem until I want to be free from it. Suffering implies a future time when I will be free from suffering, and it's a vicious circle. Nobody can end suffering.

Q. Can you repeat that? So pain is there ...

Not the idea of pain, but present sensation, moment by moment. Present! Present! Present! *(Slaps leg several times).* Now, now, now! And then the story, "Why is this happening to me?" Which implies, doesn't it, that I don't want this to be happening. But it *is* happening! Everything is just happening, presently! And it's not a problem until you want to be free from it. And in that attempt to be free, you're creating this "me". What is this "me" but a resistance to *this*?

And the mind cannot accept this. How can we accept that this is all there is?

Q. So is this just about living in the moment?

But there's always the struggle, isn't there, to live in the moment? It just becomes another search. We're *always* living in the moment. This moment *already is.* We can't *not* live in the moment!

This is a radical message. That this is it! This is everything we've ever been searching for. This is it. And all that self-improvement stuff, it's all wonderful, but it implies a tomorrow. It implies a future. It implies that this moment may not be your last. It implies a "me" that's going to be there tomorrow. This is an assumption, that we're going to be alive tomorrow! So yes, this message is really about living in the moment! This moment is all there is. It's all we have! This is your last moment! But the mind doesn't want to hear that, because it wants to have all of these projects, and it needs a future, to be free, to improve, to be happy. The mind doesn't want to stop. It wants to carry on, churning away, trying to be free, trying to be happy, and that's all fine! Until it's not. And at some point, for this character, all of that just didn't work anymore.

So all that healing and meditation stuff, it's all wonderful, and I wouldn't ever want to stop anyone from doing any of it. But this message undercuts all of that. It points to the obvious: this moment is all there is. We do not have tomorrow! That's an assumption, a story. We could get killed on the way home. It's possible! One of us could have a brain haemorrhage in the next few seconds. It's possible, it happens!

Q. I'm just wondering if I should fake it, for effect! *(Laughter)* **So "tomorrow" is an assumption?**

Yes, an assumption. Past, present and future are assumptions. Concepts. Thoughts.

Q. So if we just become more present, the mind is calmer?

But "becoming present" is just another process, another path, more of the search. "I need to be more present!". If you try and become more present, you can also apparently become less present! "Damn, I lost presence!" *(Laughter)*

Q. It becomes a burden.

Yes, a burden. And what's happened over here (and this is not an achievement) is that this search, this striving, has just been seen through. And whatever happens, happens. And it's not a problem. And the very idea of improving myself, it's just another struggle, a burden. And in the attempt to improve ourselves, or free ourselves, we're creating our very selves! All of these processes rest on the assumption that there's someone here in the first place who can do all that stuff! And this is the message: *who* is the one that's here? What reality does this "me" have?

Q. So if you're striving, you're not truly acknowledging yourself for who you really are?

You've assumed there's someone there, and that's the problem!

Q. You're saying there is no "me"?

So ... what's happening? There's the sound of the clock ticking. Not the *idea* of the sound of the clock ticking, but *that*. And there's breathing … and where's this self? I simply don't find it!

You and your life story, all the things you've done in your life, who you think you are: it all arises now as thought, doesn't it? Just a story happening now. There's no self outside of that! No "me" having thoughts of "me" – that's the illusion!

And in the story of Jeff, for example, there was meditation and self-improvement, intensely, intensely! And there were mind-blowing spiritual experiences and all sorts of things. And yet … it's all passed. It's all *past*. It's all gone. It's just a story.

Q. Yes, but it's anchored you … it's done *something* …?

No. No. It's done *nothing*. It's irrelevant. The past is irrelevant. It's a good story! It's a very good story! And the mind cannot accept this. That this is all there is! Because what happens to all our ideas of a future enlightenment, and improving ourselves … what happens to all of that if this – this moment – is it? If we're going to be happy in the *future*, if we're going to be joyful in the *future* … what happens to all of that?

Q. I think there are processes that we can do to bring us closer to the moment …

But we don't have time! We don't have that luxury! The whole idea of process, it's a nice idea but it implies that we have time!

Q. So, this is happening, everything's just happening, and there's no choice in it.

Yes, but the story of "choice" might happen. Or the story of "no choice" might happen. This message is so simple, but the mind cannot accept it, because the mind wants to carry on searching, improving, becoming. It's all the mind can do! It doesn't want to give up. And this is about the giving up. Although that "giving up" can be turned into a goal, a process. And that's how the mind perpetuates itself – always wanting, always needing. And that's fine ... until it's not.

And this is what's seen through: the idea that there's something to get in life, that there's some happiness outside of *this*, that there's some joy outside of *this*, that there's some peace outside of *this*, that there's love outside of *this*, that there's Oneness outside of *this*.

Q. If this is it, what about making plans for the future?

Oh sure, make plans, of course! But they're just assumptions! We never know what's going to happen. How the hell could I have ever known that one day I'd be sitting in front of people giving a talk on this? How ridiculous! What can we ever know? How can we ever know anything for sure? It's a comfort, of course, thinking that we know. The mind loves to know! "I know who I am, I know what the future will hold, I know that I'm not going to be hit by a car on the way home!" We just don't know.

Q. What about motivation? If this is it, why would you be motivated to do anything?

You find yourself doing things. Coming here tonight, for instance. Whatever happens, happens. But the mind will not accept that. The mind wants to know, wants to choose, wants to plan! It wants to be in control. It wants to *think* it's in control, wants to play God.

And whatever happens is not a problem ... not until there's the desire to be free from it. Anger is not a problem, pain is not a problem, sexual desires are not a problem, something catching on fire is not a problem ... until "you" come along and don't want what happens to happen. But absolutely, if there's a fire, go put it out! Don't just sit there and go "There's no fire, so I don't need to put it out!" That's ridiculous! *(Laughter).* Don't be spiritual! There's no fire? Course there's a bloody fire! Go put it out! *(Laughter).*

So, what's arising presently? It's just not a problem, until "you" come along and want to be free from it. And in that resistance, you're creating this "me" – this strong sense of who I am and what I like and so on. And there's the separation from life! This is life, and then there's "me", with my wants and desires and regrets. And then there's the search for enlightenment, the search to be *free* from this self, and that's more of the search than ever! Want to be free from yourself? Bloody hell, you're going round in circles!

And then we have these spiritual experiences where all sense of "me" dies away. And in the story of Jeff these have apparently happened... but it's not relevant at all. It doesn't mean anything. In the story, there were times when thought died away. And then thought comes back in and says "Wow, all thought died away, that was an enlightenment experience, I must be reaching enlightenment!" And then thought says "Right, I'm gonna have another one of those no-thought experiences!" *(Laughter)* And then the search for the next no-thought experience happens. And of course, only thought would search for the end of thought ...

Thoughts just happen. They're simply not a problem. There's this idea that in order to reach enlightenment we need to be free from thought. There's stories about enlightened masters who freed themselves from all thought, and we desperately want to be like them! That's the myth ...

Q. So, we have many false assumptions, and seeing those assumptions as they arise, as being false, is liberation ...

And that's not something that happens in time. That seeing is *now*. Liberation as a future possibility is just another one of those assumptions. We seem to always want something that other people apparently have. There's this idea, isn't there, that there are liberated people, enlightened people. And then there's little old "me" who is miserable and not enlightened, and "I" want what they apparently have! And that's just an extension of the lifetime's search for something more, for freedom, for peace…

Q. Once the fundamental assumption (the existence of a separate individual) has fallen, other assumptions can fall like dominoes.

That could be the story: that there is a person there who can see through all these assumptions. That's just another story. This *(claps hands)* is it! There is nothing to get, there is *nothing* to get!

Q. But that can take a while to see, can't it?

As long as you are trying to see it! As long as you're trying to get something, it will apparently take time to get. This is it! There's nothing more. We can't have anything more. It's the idea that there's something extraordinary to get in the future that makes this – what is presently happening – ordinary. As long as there's the search for the extraordinary "out there", *this* is so ordinary! How very dull this is, if you're searching for something in the future! How lacking in love this is, if you're searching for love!

Q. There's a suggestion in the literature that once this has been seen, there is an ease of living. Is that so in your experience?

If I say "yes" it sets up this "ease" as a goal, doesn't it? "I want that ease!" And that drives the search …

Q. What about spiritual paths? The Buddha had his Noble Path ....

To an individual, it may be helpful to have a "path". But really, the idea of a path just perpetuates the illusion of "me". Any path is a lie, because it implies a future, it implies there's something more than this. Where's the future? We're never guaranteed another day, another moment!

And this is very hard to accept: right now all your entire family, all your loved ones, could be dead. The entire world "out there" could have collapsed, there could be a nuclear war going on outside this room. We're not guaranteed anything. Can the mind accept this? That this whole "outside world" is just an assumption?

(Silence)

Q. Well, we're all thinking, so no! *(Laughter)*

Beyond all theories, all the books we've ever read, all our knowledge, all paths, beyond all past and future, there is this, what is presently arising. There's something happening now! And the past – the idea of you and your lives and your families and your possessions and your achievements and so on – is dead and gone. The past only arises now as thought. That's the only reality it has! Right now, all your loved ones could be dead. They could have been killed. How would you know? Right now, how would you know? You see, that's how little power the mind actually has! It's comforting to think that there's a world "out there", and it's all very knowable and stable. But it's only stories happening now, and there's nothing beyond that. How could there be? Any idea of "something beyond this" is just a story, happening here and now. Any idea of an "outside world" is a story arising here and now.

Q. But don't our thought patterns of yesterday bring us to where we are today?

No. It's almost the exact opposite. It's now, it's always now (*claps*), undeniably! You're here, now! And yes, the story arises, now, of the character, the person, the "me", who, say, became interested in nonduality and drove to this meeting tonight. But that story is just a story arising presently. And that story happens in this – Oneness, aliveness, God. And all those words just point to this (*claps*)!

Q. What about emotions? Don't they influence us?

There's the separation again: "me" versus "my emotions". Thought has created that separation. When there is anger, when anger arises, that is all there is. There's not "somebody being angry" – that is a creation of thought. Thought separates itself from anger, creates the concept "anger", creates the "me" who is angry, tells the story "I am an angry person, I want to be free from anger", and in doing so perpetuates the anger!

This is also not about "allowing" everything to happen. Who would ever allow this? It would be easy for me to sit here and tell you all to "allow the present moment". But that's just more separation, more self, more ego. The present moment *is*! Nobody can allow it! There's nothing we can do ...

Q. This is so difficult for a person to understand!

That's because the person is *trying* to understand! The person will just go round in circles. *Who* is the one who wants to reach Oneness? *Who* is the one who wants to become one with the present moment? *Who* is the one who wants enlightenment?

Q. I'd like to become one with a chocolate biscuit!
(Laughter)

As a Zen master once said, 'Nothing is left to you at this moment, but to have a good laugh'.

PART 4

REFRACTIONS

"Biting into an apple as I sit before peonies –
that's how I'll die."

- Shiki

Pain

Whoever said this message is about freedom from pain?

There is no freedom from pain. This body is nothing but a pain machine. This body will decay: cancers will ravage it, the heart will seize up, the limbs will fail, breathing will become excruciating, and freedom will seem an impossibility, a fancy story dreamt up by people with too much time on their hands. Are we ready to accept this?

Concepts like "I am not the body"- aren't these just comforting beliefs, defence mechanisms against the inevitable? In the face of intense physical pain, all attempts to rationalise or intellectualise or "understand" simply crumble: an individual cannot think pain away, no matter how hard they think, or don't think. The pain is there. It's only in the resistance to pain that the trouble begins, it's only when "I" come in, with my dislike of pain, that the pain becomes a problem.

Only humans turn pain into a problem, that is, we weave a story around what is in fact very natural for a physical organism. And then, what is really only a moment-to-moment sensation, a dynamic expression of aliveness, becomes part of a complex narrative, usually a scary one, with an uncertain duration and an often miserable conclusion.

But really, no narrative is needed: the pain is enough, and it is very real. Indeed, the pain is all there is. And "we" are nothing but the attempt to flee that pain.

We create ourselves in fleeing ourselves.

Concepts like "Pain arises for no-one" and "What is pain if it is not labelled as such?" can be very helpful. But they are still just concepts. What is real, is this burning sensation in the chest, is this crushing pain in the leg, is this throbbing in the head – not the words, but the undeniable actuality.

And in this real, intense pain, there is no suffering.

But then "I" come along and label the pain as pain, and with that, I imply that I don't want the pain to be there. I call myself a "victim" and desperately wish for a time when the present pain will be no more. I do not want this moment to be as it is.

The pain is not the problem: I am the problem. Indeed, what am I apart from all of this psychological resistance?

Meanwhile, the pain goes on.

Can anyone really accept that no matter what the spiritual teachings tell us, this body is at some point, going to fail, miserably? If it is not doing so already. Can we really accept that at some point in the future, imagined or not, there will be excruciating physical pain?

Even Jesus cried out when they nailed his wrists to the cross.

And yet, Jesus knew that this, too, was God.

This is what we've all forgotten: intense physical pain is God, as much as a beautiful sunset or an embrace from a loved one is God.

And so this message is not about a denial or transcendence of physical pain, for that is not even possible. This message is about the realisation that God is everything, literally everything. And only an individual, a "me", would think otherwise. Indeed, "thinking otherwise" is all an individual can do.

But this is not necessarily a religious message; instead of "God" you can say "Reality" or "Buddha Mind" or

"Tao" or "Spirit" or "What Is" or "Fish and Chips" or a billion other things.

What We Really, Really Want ...

You cannot have what you want, ever.

It is the wanting itself which destroys the possibility of ever having what you want, for the wanting implies that *something* can be captured and owned by *someone*. But who could ever capture, and who could ever own?

There is only this, and this can never be captured, because it is not a thing amongst other things, but the open, spacious possibility of all possibilities which gives rise to all things in the first place.

What we really want is an end to our wanting, but even the wanting of an end to wanting is another want, perhaps the biggest want of them all.

Wanting implies that there is something to get: but is there really anything to get in the first place, or was our wanting always only in vain? Perhaps the wanting obscures the obvious: we already have everything we could ever want, because right now, an end to all our wants, all our desires, all our problems is already with us, and that end is so simple: these desires, problems, wants, troubles, annoyances do not really exist, in that they are simply thoughts arising now. That's all they are, all the troubles of the world: thoughts.

And so really, what we want is an end to thought. But wouldn't that just be more thinking?

But an end to thought is not really needed. Thought happens, thought appears, and there is nobody doing it. Isn't this obvious? Thought simply appears, and so already thought is not "mine", it's not personal, it's just happening in this infinite awareness, in this open space, which is not separate from its content.

Like clouds floating through the sky, like drops of rain trickling down the window pane, thoughts aren't really a problem at all.

Thoughts are only a problem when an individual wants to be free from them. But how could an individual ever be free from thought? An individual is the very thought he seeks to be free from! It's a merry-go-round, and there's no way out for an individual seeking a way out.

And so an individual can never, ever have what he wants, because the individual is actually nothing but those wants, those desires, those problems. To be free from wants would be to die, and why would an individual ever want that?

No, there is no way out: life is just as it is, and any resistance to that actually creates the very individual who thinks he needs to be free from life and its problems. The individual is resistance, and resistance cannot end resistance.

Still, resistance may be seen. And in that seeing, there is freedom. But this is not something anyone can do.

Allowing Individuality

Language implies the subject-object split, i.e. *someone* (an individual) talking about *something*. This cannot be avoided, and therefore "nondual" language is simply a contradiction in terms: language is inherently dualistic in its binary oppositional structure.

So let's not be afraid of talking about individuals! As long as we bear in mind that individuals are only apparent individuals, in that they only "exist" as stories, as elaborate narratives, arising now.

For example, right now I could say "My name is Jeff, I'm 26 years old, I live in the UK ..." And this is true in the sense that it's a story arising now. We don't need to deny the apparent existence of the individual. It's just a play, a game: it's the incredible so-called "human drama".

And so sometimes you will hear me referring to an individual who can apparently do things: give up their prejudices, see through illusion, and so on. And this is absolutely true from the perspective of the apparent individual: they can apparently give up their prejudices and they can apparently see through illusion, and so on.

But even this is still part of the play, part of the human drama, the great game of life. It's all still just a story, a bundle of thought, arising now, and it has no more reality than that.

So let's not be afraid to talk about individuals apparently doing things! Let's talk about the human drama, about individuals apparently falling in love, apparently going shopping, apparently going on holiday, apparently fighting with each other, apparently feeling pain and rage and jealousy and joy. The individual, as I say over and over again, does not need to be denied. And only an individual would ever deny an individual anyway...

When I say things like "Let's see through our differences", I'm talking as an individual to another individual, since that's the way language is structured. But these individuals are already only stories appearing presently in awareness. They appear as thought now, now and now. In reality, these individuals don't really "exist".

This life is just a play of appearances, and there is no need to deny, negate or transcend these appearances. The appearances are fine as they are.

It's a wonderful show, for no-one. Nothing is more "spiritual" than anything else. The play of individuality is already divine, exactly as it already is.

When we use words, we speak as individuals. I sometimes find it amusing when individuals claim to be speaking from "beyond individuality" or from "impersonal awareness" or from some other wonderful state. Doesn't this just set up "liberation" or "enlightenment" as something to achieve, something that some people "have" and others do not? Does this not just encourage the search? Does this not set some people up as "teachers" and reduce others to "students"? Does this not perpetuate the violence that is supposed to be ended in "liberation"?

All of this is fine, I'm not condemning it. It's just part of the great game of life. But the game already arises now, for no-one, and the whole student-teacher drama is simply another part of the show, with no deeper reality. Really, there are no students and no teachers; those are just stories.

Right now, in this moment, life already simply appears! What else do we need? I'd be wary of any individual (apparent or otherwise) who claims you need to do something to "get" this.

How can we "get" this when this is already fully present, right now?

How can we "get" this when we *are* this?

Death

Upon death, only the story of "me" is lost. Only the story of an individual dies, and what remains was never born in the first place.

Only the story of "me" ever enters the stream of time. Indeed, this narrative creates time as we know it. And so at the point of death, what falls away is time itself. That is to say, at the point of death, all that is false dissolves into the nothingness that embraces all truth and falsehood, the nothingness that is not separate from everything that arises.

Which is to say, a person dies, that is undeniable, but that in which the person arises in the first place is indestructible, because it is not part of the apparent world of time and space.

Death is already here, for all of us, because death is not separate from what we are. As long as there is the belief that death is something that will happen to "me" in the future, then death is exactly that: something that will happen to "me" in the future. Thought creates world.

And so, let's celebrate death. It is not the enemy. It

(apparently) comes to an individual when it comes, and indeed, from a certain standpoint, it is the only certainty in life.

From another standpoint, there is no death at all.

And from another, death is this.

And really, there are no standpoints at all.

Everything simply arises and dissolves in this open space, this vastness which holds all manifestation. "I" arise in this vastness, and the story "I am a separate individual" arises too, as does the story "One day I will die". And no matter what arises or dissolves, the vastness remains untouched, always. The vastness accepts everything, unconditionally, *including* the arising and dissolving of the individual, that is, including my apparent life and my apparent death.

And so, "you" will never really die, because "you" were never really born. There is *only* this wide open space in which all ideas about birth, life and death arise and dissolve. And so all is well, because all your problems, and indeed all the problems of the world, are just stories arising in this vastness, a vastness which allows everything to be exactly as it already is.

Yes, *all is well*. In the pain and the sadness, the joy and the madness, all is well. And death was always just a story told to frighten us.

Perhaps This Is Love

Why do we all pretend to be separate from each other?

The ground of all things is love. And yet we erect boundaries and divisions, and then claim that these boundaries and divisions are part of the natural order of things, denying our praxis and giving weight to the illusion of an objective world "out there", when of course the world, as every child knows, was "in here" all along.

And with this illusory separation comes anxiety, loneliness, and boredom. But perhaps that is a blessing, because perhaps, in the midst of frustration and despair, a new possibility will arise.

Or perhaps not.

Anyhow, you only have to look at this world we have created to be reminded that there is something wrong. People, for the most part, are scared, rigid, closed-in, set in their ways. They see themselves as pawns of fate in a deterministic universe, and for most of their lives this is how they live, as if the world "out there" (whatever that means) had some bearing on who and what they are now.

Well, it's a nice illusion.

Right now, who are you?

Right now, in who or what are these words being perceived?

Who, in this moment, is aware of the sights and sounds in the room?

You? And what is "you"? Are you the "you" you were five years ago? Are you the "you" you were when you were a child? Has this "you" changed? And who is aware of this change?

You see, right now, there are sights and sounds and smells, and with them, an idea of yourself as an individual, a person, an entity of some kind with a past and a future.

But in who or what does all this arise, now? If you're honest, radically so, you'll have to admit this: *There is no-one there.* There are sights and sounds and smells (not the words, not the concepts, but the actual reality to which these words point, that is, present sights, present sounds, present smells) but there is simply nobody there seeing, hearing and smelling. Only purest sensation, and nothing more. And then the idea "I am seeing, I am hearing, I am smelling" may arise, but this is to beg the question – who is at the centre of all this?

And what about apparent others? Let's see: someone appears on the scene, and there is the thought "Here is another person, another individual, just like me, but separate from me."

And there the violence begins.

In reality, when "someone else" appears, I have no idea what it is in front of me. And then this person speaks, and two individuals appear to be having what's known as a "conversation". But is there really any separation between us? Is this separation not just a construction of thought? Are we not the same, you and me?

But the world goes on, and with it, the illusion of separation. We live our lives as though we are separate. And with that comes isolation, loneliness, anxiety, the desire to be popular, the desperation to succeed over everyone else. Separation is violence, and violence is separation. Could the Holocaust have been possible if the Nazis hadn't promoted the idea that Jews were very different from Aryans? Was separation and us-and-them thinking not at the root of it all? Is this not true for all wars and genocides?

Right now, because there is no "me", there is no "you" either. Yes, these ideas may arise, but they arise now, and they arise for no-one. They float in awareness, along with all the sights and sounds in the room, including the image of your apparent body. "You" are just an idea to me (though this is not to deny the body, and the apparent sounds you emit, and so on).

Perhaps this division will never be healed, I don't know. But the world goes on, and the insanity of violence goes along with it. And the violence is part of the very fabric of what we take to be ourselves. The violence cannot be healed by practising what we call "love". Only when the violence dissolves (is seen through) perhaps, then, do we have a chance.

Love is not something we do, love is something we are, but this is apparently obscured by the illusion of separation. Of course, it's never really ever obscured – it is always here, we are always it. Perhaps in our quest to "be someone" in this world, we forgot. Perhaps as children we knew the truth: this, this moment, is all we have. In this moment, and this moment alone, we are one. Separation is only the illusion of past and future.

Perhaps this is love: this moment, and everything that arises in it.

Just perhaps.

Who Cares?

What is "understanding",
but the falling away
of all attempts
to "understand"?

What is "knowing",
but the dissolution
of the one who
wants to "know"?

What is "enlightenment",
but the seeing-through
of the very idea of
"enlightenment"?

What is "liberation",
but the end of liberation
as "we" know it?

What is the search for liberation
but a fun little game
we play with ourselves?

And what is this fun little game
but a story
arising now?

What is anything
but a story
arising now,
for no-one?

A story arising
in this open space
which allows everything,

in this nothingness
which accepts all forms,
effortlessly,
choicelessly,
presently,
simply.

And what are these words
but another
futile attempt
to talk about
this?

No words
are necessary.

No words
have ever
been necessary.

But hey,
talking about this
can be fun.

Yes, fun!

If words come, who cares?
If they don't, who cares?

Full Stop

Yes! This is an emptiness, but it is an emptiness full to the brim with sights and sounds and smells.

And it's all so ordinary, so obvious.

Having a shit,

Brushing your teeth,

Being ravaged by cancer,

Screaming with pain in the middle of the night.

That is it too.

For so long "I" wanted to be free from all that pain and suffering.

But "I" didn't realise that "I" was nothing *but* that demand to be free from pain, to be free from life, to be free from myself.

Haha!

It was that very demand to be free, which was creating the one who wanted to be free.

No matter. It's all over now. And it never really began in the first place.

Just this. Nothing more. Full stop.

Silent Sermon

Out of nothing,
out of purest silence
a world appears.

And the world
is not separate from the silence,
and the silence
is not separate from the world.

And who knows this?

To say "There is no self"
or to say "There is a self"
or to say "The self is illusion"
or to say anything at all
(and to say even that)
is already to say
too much.

Anything that can be said
is not it,
but then again
not saying anything
is not it either.

Nor is saying
that it cannot be spoken of.

Beyond the words,
beyond the teachings of men,
beyond any experience a person could ever have,
beyond all memories of the past and ideas about the future,
what is real?

This, this is real.

This moment.

Not the idea of it,
not the thought of it,
but this –
(and here is where words completely fail)
– this present appearance:

Tap-tapping of the keys,
Hum of the laptop fan,
Breathing
A car beeping its horn
Floorboards creaking.

There is simply nothing else to understand.

The idea that there is something to understand makes it seem like there is something to understand.

But there is nothing to understand.

Wise men telling you that there is something to understand and reading book after book about how there is something to understand can make it seem like there is something to understand.

But **this** cannot be understood.

This is already this.

See, it's simple.

Remember the Buddha's silent sermon. He said nothing, but held up a flower to his audience. Only Kasyapa smiled, whilst everyone else looked confused.

Kasyapa "got it" because he knew there was nothing to get.

There was only the flower. When you're seeking for something other than the flower, you do not really see the flower. Kasyapa saw the flower, and it pleased him. So simple. So obvious.

PART 5
AND THERE WAS A WORLD

"And everywhere, infinite options, infinite possibilities.
An infinity, and at the same time, zero.
We try to scoop it all up in our hands,
and what we get is a handful of zero."

- Haruki Murakami, *The Elephant Vanishes*

Genesis

And the Earth was without form, and void; and darkness was upon the face of the deep...

This morning, the eyes opened, and there was a world. Incarnation. Spirit made flesh. There was something new under the Sun, something that had never been there before, something that could never be there again. A world had been thrown out of the Void, something had emerged from nothing. I looked around. There was a room. Curtains, a cupboard, a stack of books, a chest of drawers. Two feet dangling off the edge of the bed.

This was a new world, an undiscovered country. Nothing in the history of the cosmos could compare to this.

How could any of it be possible? How could there be something? Anything?

The duvet was thrown off the bed. A body appeared: the first body, the first man, Adam himself. Two legs, two arms, and the rest. A miracle had occurred! Creation *ex nihilo!* But it was a dynamic, restless miracle: the body moved, first to eat breakfast, then into the bathroom to wash itself, then to the door. Nothing could stop the miracle from unfolding. The miracle was everything.

Outside, there was a bitter wind that chilled the face. The body boarded a bus. That is, I boarded the bus, but there was no I, and no bus, and certainly no body that could possibly board any bus. But still, I boarded that bus. And on the bus, the miracle continued. I looked around. There were others, others like me! Arms and legs and torsos and heads with funny little scrunched up faces, some smiling, some gazing into the middle distance, some filled with the sorrow of the world. But they were my brothers and sisters, all of them! We were all the same, there was nothing to divide us at all, absolutely nothing. One family under the burning sun, bound together in more profound ways than we ever could imagine.

We were all one, which is to say there was nobody at all on that bus, nobody at all. And yet, there were those bodies, that was undeniable.

And I got off the bus, and walked around the town centre. Humanity throbbed. Thousands of people packed into shops, bustling around bus stops, chatting on benches, drinking coffee from little paper cups with fancy logos. Lovers embracing, husbands and wives quarrelling, bus engines roaring, children playing hide-and-seek.

What *were* these creatures? And how was it possible that I had woken up this morning as one of them? What had I ever done to deserve it? I caught my reflection in a shop window. Oh, the miracle of the human face! The miracle of arms, of legs, of a unique appearance distinguishing me from the others, whilst at the same time binding me to them forever ...

And though we were all wrapped up warmly in our winter clothes, I knew that the miracle went even deeper. Under these clothes that marked us out as seemingly separate individuals, there were things that bound us inherently to each other, things that marked us all out as of the same blood. Dirty things, shameful things, secret things. Penises, vaginas, breasts, sweat, urine, blood, pus. Cancers, incontinence, missing limbs, growths, deformities. We try to cover these things up, but today I could see through the disguises, today I saw our common humanity, and it was almost too beautiful to bear. I saw the lies and half-lies and half-truths and props and masks that we used to divide ourselves from each other, to hide ourselves, and I saw how these things only ever served to make us more human, to disclose exactly that which we sought so desperately to hide. Yes, today I saw through all of that, I saw to the heart of what it meant to be human, of what it meant to be alive on this day; on this day of all days.

And what I saw was nothing more than what met the eyes, and what I heard was nothing more than what met the ears. What I saw was so obvious, so painfully obvious, so obviously present, that it was perhaps another miracle that we all didn't see it, all of us, all of the time.

And yet, that day I really saw nothing, for there was no

I to see anything at all.

It was growing dark now. The body was becoming tired. There was hunger and thirst. I boarded the bus back home. Still the miracle, still the miracle. Always the miracle.

A key in the lock. Light switches flicked on. Shoes off.

Today I lived my entire life, without remainder, and now there is nothing else to do, nowhere else to go. It is night-time, and I find myself back here, in my bed, where the world first appeared this morning. Perhaps a world will appear tomorrow. I don't know. For now, just this is enough. Just this is the miracle.

Today I lived my entire life, but it has already faded into memory, back into the void from whence it came.

Today I lived my entire life, and as I lie here beneath my duvet on the verge of sleep, no less comfortable than I was in my mother's womb, I am ready for death, the Womb of all Wombs.

But for now, there will be sleep. And tomorrow, there may be a world.

And the eyes close, and the world dissolves.

Nothing Ever Happens

Nothing ever happens. Everything passes before the eyes, and nothing stays. From moment to moment, there is no build up, no residue: each moment is an entirely new world, and any similarity to the previous world is an illusion, an illusion which gives rise to the idea of permanence, of there being some entity here who carries himself from the past to the future. But there is no such entity, only the passing of content through awareness now, now and now, an awareness which is identical with that content.

And so nothing ever happens. "Something happening" is a story, a tale, arising now, a story without a storyteller, a tale told by no-one, a tale *full of sound and fury, signifying nothing.*

There is only this: flashes of colour, bursts of sound, passing sensations, varying temperatures, smells hitting the nostrils. Only this, and nothing more. Only this, and nothing ever to show for it.

Like sand passing through fingers, this life cannot be grasped. In fact, the more we try to grasp it, the less "alive" we really are.

Although really we can never be more or less alive. We are life, and anything we do, or don't do, is still a perfect expression of life, of Oneness.

There's no escape from this. None whatsoever.

Coming Home

This is timeless, deathless, eternal.

This is without equal, this is never-to-be-repeated, this is utterly unique and totally new, in each and every moment, although there are no "moments" at all.

This is empty of all qualities, even the quality of being empty of all qualities. And yet, this is totally full, pregnant with infinite possibility, possibility that overflows again and again into a world.

This is peace, but it is a volcanic peace, a peace which does not deny noise but embraces it fully, a peace which does not rest, an ecstatic peace that throws itself out of itself now, now and now.

This is completely unknowable, and yet it is filled with the knowledge of things, filled with an apparent world "out there", in its infinite guises.

This is something that cannot be spoken of by anyone, and yet words are thrown out, day after day after day.

This is not of this world, and yet it is nothing *but* this world.

This is completely extraordinary, and yet it is as simple

and as obvious as the sound of the rain *splish-splashing* on your rooftop.

Splish! Splash!

This is a wide open space, with enough room for an entire world, pulsating with a radical and unconditional love that will never be grasped by a mind locked in the search for something more.

This is simple, obvious, ordinary.

This is what everybody is seeking, but nobody can find.

And nobody can find this precisely because the one who searches for this is exactly that which apparently obscures this (although this can never be obscured, because it already includes any idea of a somebody who would want something more).

This is Jesus dying on the cross.

This is the Buddha seeing through all confusion.

This is the world falling away when two lovers embrace.

This is a mother cradling her newborn child.

This is watching an old man waddling down the pavement, and seeing only yourself.

This is your heart breaking at the sight of an old woman, her shopping bags full of groceries, struggling to cross a busy road, and finding yourself, without hesitation, rushing over to help her, because you have no choice, and you never did have any choice.

And this is realising, at long last, that choice is illusion, that you were never *for one moment* separate from this thing we call "life", that we were never *for one moment* separate from each other; that no man is an island, that we affect each other in more profound ways than the mind could ever hope to grasp.

The Mystery of Things

This world only has any meaning because there is a "me" (apparent or otherwise) for whom it has any meaning. Which is to say, there is no world outside of "my" world. This is not a descent into solipsism, or nihilism, nor a denial of reality of any kind, but a description of what is actually and quite obviously the case.

The thing in front of me that I call a "mug", for example, has meaning for me: it is something that holds my hot drinks, something I have used in the past and will most probably continue to use in the future. In a very real sense, this mug is part of me, part of what I take to be myself. What I take to be myself cannot in any way be separated from the concept "mug".

"Mug" has meaning for me on a multitude of levels. There are associations with my past; I can remember friends and acquaintances using mugs; I have my favourite mug, it has a special relevance for me; I remember when I had my first cup of tea in a mug, and how, throughout my childhood, my mother would always take her coffee in a mug, while my father would insist on having his tea in a cup and saucer. Mugs have provided me with great pleasure over the years: I have had countless cups of tea and coffee, day after day. All of this very personal meaning is contained in the word "mug". How can I separate myself from the idea of a "mug", then? And how can

I separate myself from this particular mug in front of me?

This mug exists for me and me alone: I give it meaning, I give it value, I give it purpose. Without this projection of values, I have no way of knowing what this thing in front of me actually is. Without this projection, this knowledge, these associations, I would be discovering this overwhelmingly mysterious thing in front of me for the very first time. "Mug" – the knowledge of it – gives me certainty and familiarity, gives me some sense of permanence and continuity in a mysterious and frightening world.

Not just the mug, though, but all things: all things are part of me, I give meaning to all things, give value, give a history and future. They arise and dissolve with me. And therefore we come to the shattering conclusion (and it is not really a conclusion at all): *I am the world, and the world is me*, something which J. Krishnamurti was fond of saying. Which is to say, there is no world "out there" at all. That is the primary illusion. No, there is no world out there, because this – right here, right now – is the world in its entirety. There is simply no need to postulate a world "outside". And even if there was, it would only be a present projection. I would have to give it meaning now, I would have to quite literally create it out of nothing in this very moment, this apparent outside world. And even if that was at all possible, it would still be my world, it would still, literally, be my very own self.

The self-other dichotomy is a false one, for everything is self, in that everything is given meaning only because there is a so-called human reality. Indeed, there must first be a human reality in order for the self-other dichotomy to come into being, and to be given any meaning.

So where does this leave us? It leaves us in a world which is no longer alien, no longer full of strangers, no longer cold and uncaring, but a world which is a friend, a lover even, full of nothing but our own projections, our own images, full of nothing but mind. We see mind wherever we look; indeed, *to look is to see mind*. There is nowhere it is not; there is nowhere we are not.

So, to look around the world, to walk about and to interact with apparent things and apparent others is to be completely and madly in love. And to be completely and madly in love with all things is to end all violence, inner and outer, because violence is nothing but separation, and separation is nothing but violence. When all is self, when there are no others, when the self-other split is healed, when there is total selfishness (which is total selflessness, however paradoxical that may sound to the rational mind), there is a love and an equanimity which permeates everything and everyone, which saturates all interactions between all apparent others; a love which was always there in the first place, a love we'd perhaps just forgotten for a while.

Look at all the things that surround you: the towel which only has any meaning because it is the towel you have used to dry yourself every morning; the chair which only has any meaning because you have sat on it countless times, resting your body after a weary day at the office; the kitchen sink which only has any meaning because you have washed up your dirty plates and cutlery in it, bathing your hands in its warm soapy water, scrubbing the knives and forks and spoons until they reflected an entire world.

You have lived this life, *you* have become familiar with these things, *you* have made your own unique sense out of them.

You own this world, you make it, you bring it into existence out of nothing. You are a magician, a sorcerer, a god even, taking an emptiness and filling it with meaning and purpose and a sense of past and future.

You take emptiness and fill it up with yourself.

And so, if the world is cruel and uncaring in your eyes then *you* have made it that way. If the world is lacking in love and compassion, then it is your responsibility, and yours alone, to bring love and compassion back into it. If there is violence in the world, that is because there is violence in you.

This is your world, and it will end when you end.

This is your day, this is your moment, this is your last chance to experience anything at all. Right now, right here, reading these words, this is all there is. This is the beginning and end of all things, this is the Alpha and the Omega, this is who and what you are, this is it, and there is nothing more, and there never was anything more.

Your whole life, all your hopes and dreams and ambitions and goals: everything comes down to this.

Sitting on the toilet. Attending the funeral of a loved one. Listening to Mozart. Reading your favourite book. Screaming with pain in the middle of the night. Crying your eyes out. Laughing so hard your stomach hurts. Being diagnosed with cancer. Holding a newborn baby in your arms, looking deep into its gorgeous little eyes, shocked and saddened for a moment by the beauty and the sacredness and the fragility of this overwhelmingly mysterious thing we call "life".

Wherever You Go …

Wherever you go, there you are. Which is to say that "you" don't really go anywhere at all, ever.

Sitting on the train, travelling across the country to visit my parents, the clarity is there: "I" am simply not travelling anywhere; if anything, the world is travelling through me. The trees and buildings speed past, but this arises in an open space, which is not separate from who or what I am.

And so although I am apparently travelling on a train, I cannot find an "I" travelling anywhere (and yet, if someone comes up and asks me, I might say that yes, I am indeed travelling …). And this is not some "state" I have achieved, this is simply the utterly obvious revealing itself: *wherever you go, there you are.* It is always here, always now, and whatever you are is not separate from all that arises.

And so I get off the train, having travelled halfway across the country, and yet I am still home. And I am always home, because home is always here, always now. In the middle of a battlefield, in a supermarket, in a gas chamber, in a spaceship, it's still here, and it's still now, and I am always all that arises, moment to moment.

This is not clever wordplay: this is the actuality of

things. Have you ever had any experience which was not now? Have you ever heard a sound that wasn't a present sound? Ever had a memory that wasn't a memory arising presently?

All life is now, and yet we live in an apparent world, as apparent characters with apparent pasts and futures, and all of this implies a yesterday and a tomorrow. And that's fine – it's the human drama. But the human drama arises now, doesn't it? It arises in this, this open space, this nothingness which paradoxically contains all things. Although it doesn't really "contain" things at all, since it's not a container. It is all things. Nothingness is fullness, and so nothingness and fullness really point to nothing but this, this present arising, these present sights, smells, thoughts, sensations …

And so although I have travelled halfway across the country, I haven't really moved at all.

There Is Nothing to Understand!

To try and put this into words is impossible, futile; no, it's laughable! How to point to the absolute miracle of existence, the awesome gift that is each and every single moment? The world, apparent or otherwise, is indescribably beautiful, sometimes painfully so. The simple fact that anything is happening at all, sometimes it's all just too much, and it often renders me speechless, or monosyllabic at least. If you're trying to talk to me, it might appear as though I am being rude. No, it's just that I cannot find any words for this miracle that we call "life". I simply cannot bring myself to *reduce* it to words ...

Oh, I cannot play the game any longer, the game where we're all supposed to pretend that we're "people", "individuals", somehow separate from each other, somehow abstracted from this moment, from this present happening, from this, this and this. How the hell could I talk about *myself*, even if I wanted to? How could I speak about something that isn't even there, that doesn't even exist? And if I did manage to speak, who the hell would be doing the speaking? And what would I talk about?

Sometimes silence is the only option.

Why do we need to talk, anyway? Why do we need to refer to a past that is dead and gone, to a future that is yet to come? Why can't we just sit together, as friends, as lovers, and gasp, together, at this awesome spectacle unfolding quite literally all around us? How is it all happening? Where does it all come from? How is it even possible, for all this to arise out of nothing?

To stare the world in the face, as it unfolds, is to be annihilated. No wonder we fill the void with our stories; to surrender to this is to die, and that, understandably, is the last thing "we" want. But oh, to die into this! To be annihilated, to dissolve into the nothingness! The nothingness that we already are!

Why do we spend our lives resisting the utterly inevitable? Why do we turn life into a chore, a problem? Why are we afraid to become nothing, to see the absolute truth behind all things? And the absolute truth is that there is no truth, there is only this, that we swim in a sea of nothingness, a void, empty of all meaning and value and truth. And that is quite literally terrifying to an individual trying to be someone, trying to get somewhere; but for goodness' sake, the individual is an illusion, the individual is a damn lie, it's nothing more than a story arising now, now, and now! And how can that have any bearing on anything whatsoever?

Words confuse what is so utterly simple! Words try to make the mystery understandable, they try to make this tremendous thing we call life palatable, they try to reduce everything to concepts, ideas, abstractions. But life is beyond all abstractions! Life is happening already (look around you!). It's already arising presently, and words cannot even begin to touch that! How can we "understand" what is so utterly obvious and utterly present? Any understanding implies there is something to understand! There is nothing to understand, quite literally nothing, there is just this!

But the play of life goes on: there is colour and form and light and sound, and there is an *apparent* individual who *apparently* lives and acts in the *apparent* world. But it's all a play of appearances, and because of that it's so utterly beautiful, *painfully* so. And this beauty is an empty beauty, it is a beauty known by nobody, seen by nobody, wanted by nobody, remembered by nobody. It is a painful beauty with nobody who experiences pain or beauty, but it is a painful beauty nonetheless.

This will never be understood, and this will never be communicated, to anyone. I really don't know why I bother writing anymore.

But the words come, as they always have. And perhaps these words, pitiful abstractions though they are, may help to "point" to something beyond themselves.

I don't know. It's not for me to worry about anymore.

There is only love, only that has any meaning at all. All else is illusion.

The Kingdom of Heaven

How incredible each moment is. How undeniable: *this is this, this is here, this is now.*

What a privilege, to sit here, with the entire world appearing right before my eyes, eyes that are not really "mine" at all.

This takes no effort. No knowledge. This is not something to be attained.

This is utterly obvious presence, utterly present obviousness.

How could I have missed this my entire life?

The world simply appears. Nothing to do, nothing that needs to be done. Already this is the liberation that is sought.

How perfectly everything unfolds, moment to moment. Pain and pleasure, joy and suffering, the mesmerising play of the opposites, the great game of life, all unfolding now, now, and now, with nobody here to witness it. Indeed, any witness would be part of the show.

No need to deny anything. No need to deny pain, or pleasure, or self, or no-self, or seeking, or not seeking, or enlightenment or liberation or any other concept. Not at all. Everything is welcome here. Everything appears effortlessly. There is neither volition nor lack of it, neither choice nor lack of it, neither destiny nor lack of it. Nothing to be, nowhere to go, nothing to be said, nobody here who could possibly say anything.

And yet the words come, as they always have. Where they come from: that is the divine mystery.

And over here, the desire to "solve" the mystery has simply faded away.

And if there is seeking, that is fine (although there is nothing to find).

If there is pain, that is fine too (although nobody feels it).

If there is frustration, that is fine as well (but what is frustration when it is not known as frustration?).

If there is anything at all, that is fine. Only the desire for this not to be as it is would apparently distract. And yes, apparent distraction is fine too.

Everything is already fine: the play accommodates it all.

Even the play not being seen as a play: that is fine. There's nobody that could possibly see the play as a play, anyway. And even if they could, it would already be part of the play.

We are always here. We never left here. Perhaps we were confused for a while. No matter. We're still here, and it's still now. The utterly obvious can never leave us.

Breathing.

Heart beating.

Coldness in the hands.

Hunger arising in the belly.

All is accepted. Everything is allowed. Anything is possible.

Everything already arises spontaneously. Everything is already accepted by no-one. This is unconditional love: acceptance without conditions. The acceptance of all manifestation. And this is already true for all of us. Everything is already accepted, because everything already arises spontaneously, effortlessly. The effort to "accept" would deny the acceptance that we are.

How beautiful this is, moment to moment. How unpredictable, how mysterious, how vibrant.

The colours of the autumn leaves.

Crunching those leaves beneath my feet.

The chill of the wind.

The dew on the flowers.

The low hum of traffic.

Why do we search for Heaven when we are already here, all of the time? Heaven in the midst of pain, Heaven in bereavement and death and war, Heaven in the good times as well as the bad times. As long as there is seeking, there is the implication that Heaven is somewhere else, in some other place, at some other time. And that's fine, that's Heaven too.

But why search in the first place? This body is decaying. Indeed, we are not even guaranteed another day. Not even another moment. This could be our last moment. Really, truly, we don't know.

This could be your last moment. So why seek? Not that there's anything wrong with it. But what are you looking for? And when will you find it?

Could what you are looking for be right in front of you?

Literally, right in front of your eyes?

Is that possible?

And his disciples said to him:
"On what day will the Kingdom come?"
And Jesus replied:
"It will not come while people watch for it;
they will not say 'Look, here it is!' or 'Look, there it is!,'
but the Kingdom of Heaven is spread out over the earth,
and people do not see it."

The Robin

Nothing to hold onto anymore.
Nothing tangible.

No safety net.

No security.

No comforting beliefs.

Nothing. No-thing.

Void.

And in that Void, everything.

An empty fullness, a full emptiness.

And beyond these words, beyond these strange little squiggles that symbolise nothing beyond themselves, beyond all philosophies, beyond the intellect, beyond all attempts to understand, beyond the absolutely futile attempt to put all of this into words, beyond even these words being read right now, beyond it all, there is a little *robin* in the tree over there, and I have no idea what he is doing, or why he is there, or why any of this is happening at all (and there is undeniably something going on!), but I expect that the little robin has never struggled with life the way humans do, he has never for a moment tried to intellectualise it all, tried to figure it out, tried to understand it, and certainly, I expect, he has never tried to escape it.

And beyond all words, all thoughts, all beliefs, all ideologies, there is that robin over there (and I say "robin" but really I haven't got the faintest idea what it is), and that robin, chirping to himself as he hops from branch to branch, singing his little song, reminds us all that there is simply nothing to get, that the idea that there is something to get is at the root of all human misery and confusion, that this present appearance is all there is or ever was, which is not a problem until "you" arrive and want it to be other than what it is.

The robin understands. Or rather, it wouldn't ever occur to him to *try* to understand. He jumps about on the tree, chirping his little song of joy and heartache, and that is the world, that is his world, and there is no other.

Oh, little robin, you know this: *nothing matters.*

And precisely because nothing matters, everything matters absolutely.

The Play of Appearances

Image upon image upon image, appearance after appearance after appearance. No end to this crazy show, no point at which life ceases and some sort of "enlightenment" happens. No desire for this to happen, even if it could. Who would want an end to this life anyway? Only an apparent someone. But is it not this apparent someone that is seen through?

Image upon image: apparent people having apparent conversations about apparent problems with the apparent outside world, apparently being frustrated at their apparent lack of power in the face of it all.

Appearance after appearance: me and you and our apparent life stories; going to work, coming home, doing the dishes, taking out the trash, buying food from the supermarket, going to the toilet, paying the bills, cleaning the house, getting ill and getting old and writhing in the most excruciating pain. No end to it all, no point at which life ceases.

This is life, and life is this. No explanation required, only the present happening presently, happening in a vastness that accepts everything, including the lack of acceptance known as "I".

"I" already arise in this vastness, and so there is nothing

more that needs to be done.

"I" am already a fiction, arising presently, and anything "I" could ever do would just be more of the fiction.

There is no escape from the fiction. No movement is possible from the "unreal" to the "real". That's just a nice story which perpetuates the search.

The unreal is as real as the real. And what does this mean?

It means the heart beating *presently*, the sound of breathing *presently*, the table and chairs and floor and ceiling of this room appearing *presently*, feelings in the body appearing *presently*.

It means this obvious present appearance, which is not something "I" could ever get closer to, or "understand" better, or "know" more intimately, because already "I" am an appearance in this totality, and a present appearance could never become anything other than a present appearance. It's all a present appearance. All of it.

And with that, the whole damn thing is over.

No more searching, or lack of it. Just this.

And this has always been the case. The search for something "more" was the very thing that created "me" as I knew myself. This is why a seeker will never be able to free himself from the search.

Words will never capture it, the absolute freedom of this, the undeniable and mind-blowing clarity that is life itself ... and yet, the utter ordinariness and simplicity of it all, and how a mind locked in the search will never understand.

Love

To confine love to that which falls within boundaries is not to love at all. To confine love is to possess, and to possess is to destroy. We destroy each other in the name of love, and the heart remains unfulfilled.

We possess each other because we are afraid to lose each other, and yet in truth there are no others, only images. We cling to these images for dear life. But love is the death of the image, and with it, the death of you and me.

We dissolve into each other, you and me. We become what we already were: *whole*. Only then do we truly see the one who is in front of us. Only then do I really see you.

To love fully, to love wholeheartedly, is to love beyond all boundaries, all notions of right and wrong, of good and bad, of this and that, of you and I. To love truly is to love without restriction, without temporal limitation, and finally, without fear.

To love fully, is to die.

And then perhaps, in love, God will look back at me through your eyes, and it will be undone, all of it. And your eyes will be my eyes, and your mouth will be my mouth, and the body will dissolve into the open space that embraces us all. No eyes, no ears, no tongue, no nose, no throat. No thing. Finally, nothing.

Perhaps only then should we dare to call it "love".

An Evening Walk

The vastness annihilates me. It literally destroys me. Walking through these empty streets, the vastness is there, consuming everything, every thought, every sensation. And yet the vastness is not separate from everything that is arising: the glow of the streetlamps, the shadows of lovers walking arm-in-arm, the rumble of night buses, the sound of footsteps on the cold pavement. And once again the secret that is so utterly obvious reveals itself: I am nowhere to be found, and I am everywhere. I am nothing, and yet I am one with all things, because there are not really any separate "things" at all.

Now, thought is silent, and yet the miracle reveals itself, all around. There is nowhere that the miracle is not. The miracle is this, this and this too. Not the idea of it, but the obvious and undeniable present actuality. Who could deny these present sights, sounds, smells? Who would ever want to?

I am annihilated in this, I am dwarfed by the vastness, I am made totally insignificant by the smallest detail: the little cracks in the pavement, the flicker of a streetlamp, a dog barking, the trees rustling in the evening breeze. Every little thing puts an end to me.

The eyes dart about, and with each movement of the eyeballs there is a new world, an undiscovered country.

Nothing is the same from one moment to the next, which is to say there are no "moments" at all. Only this, only the utterly obvious revealing itself now, now and now.

And thought is not there: thought comes afterwards, thought is always an interpretation in hindsight, a useless addition, after-the-fact. Thought is dead – this is alive. Thought is of the past – this is so clearly present. This obliterates the past, this destroys it totally. How useless the past is! How useless are those little stories, the ones about "me and my life"! They too are annihilated with every footstep, with every breath. Every moment new, every moment fresh, every moment a revelation, a miracle beyond all words.

And so, I walk alone, homeless, faceless, hopeless, without a past, without a future, without beliefs. And yet these things may arise, and that is fine. These things may arise, and if they do, who cares? Really, who gives a shit? Whatever arises, arises. Whatever happens, happens. And we only suffer to the extent that we don't want what happens to happen.

But beyond all ideas of suffering, beyond all thought, beyond any idea of "liberation" or "enlightenment" or "awakening", beyond all beyonds, those streetlights are flickering, and the wind is picking up, and there is hunger, and the body moves towards the bus stop, and presumably it's time to go home.

Consumed by the vastness, there is no longer anything to do, nowhere to go, no possibility of anything whatsoever. There is only this, as there always has been. *Nothing has changed and everything has changed*, but even that is saying too much. Nothing can be known about this. Nothing can really be said, although the words come again. And that's wonderful. Wonderful because it can't possibly be any other way.

Tonight the silence consumed me, and the silence was everything, but in the silence a world arose, and yes, it was an apparent world, but what an apparent world it was! An apparent world, apparent to no-one.

Although, in the story, I have walked through the city a hundred times before, this night was the first night I had ever walked through the city, no doubt about it. Tonight, the city was new, it was truly an undiscovered country. Nothing was known about it. Nothing. And so it wasn't really a "city" at all, not at all. It was everything. It was the universe in its fullness. And it was nothing. A vast emptiness, an empty vastness. And I was fully annihilated by the vastness, and fully present too. And there was no contradiction, none whatsoever. Contradictions arise only for a mind seeking something.

But there is no mind, and no search.

Only this, extraordinary this, undeniable this ....

.... and nothing more.

Night

And the day fades away, and there is silence.

And everything that has arisen from the silence will now fall back into the silence. And I am nowhere to be found.

And yet, and yet, there is typing of these words. And there are sounds, too: the hum of the computer fan, the boiler clicking and whooshing, my flatmate treading on the floorboards, the faint rumble of cars outside. And tingles in the body, and the *thump-thump* of the heart, and everything else that pretends to be a world.

If the world is anywhere, it is here, right here in this room. Although it's not really a room at all: it's the entire universe in its fullness. Why do we have to lie and call it a "room"? That makes it sound so small, so insignificant. But this is totally significant, because it is quite literally all there is!

And really, all these words are just bullshit. They claim to describe a world "out there" (as opposed to "in here") when the words themselves have created that division in the first place. All language is circular. Words claim that they have been written by somebody, but I can find nobody here writing these words, and certainly nobody who knows what any of the words actually *mean*.

And yet, the character "Jeff" is very much a part of this appearance. The character "Jeff" apparently got up this morning, apparently went to work, apparently came home, and is apparently now sitting in a chair, writing these words.

But "Jeff" is just another elaborate appearance in this great play. He has no greater reality than that.

What a relief, to be free from myself! What a burden it was for all those years, pretending to be an individual with a heavy past and an uncertain future. What a strain, to have to "find my way" in life, to have to pursue my interests, to have the need to forge strong relationships with people like myself, to succeed in both my career and "private life" (and how private my life used to be!).

And yet, these days, there is still apparently a "Jeff" who apparently does all those things. It's just that perhaps it's all been seen as a play, a game, a dance. And what a complex and beautiful dance it is! A dance that includes pleasure as well as pain, joy as well as heartache, health as well as illness. Anything can happen in the play of life.

And the play arises in this silence, this silence of all silences, and falls back into it, continually, endlessly, without rhyme or reason or purpose or meaning. And yet, everything is intrinsically purposeful, and drenched with meaning.

Meaning or no meaning, purpose or no purpose - no difference, truly.

But beyond all these words, there is always **this**, the undeniable present, in which the words arise in the first place. Sitting here, in my comfortable chair, everything appears, freely, effortlessly, choicelessly.

Just open your eyes, and an entire world appears, without asking anything of you. Isn't this a gift? For nothing, we get a world. And not just now, but now, now, and now too! In each and every moment we're given a world, for free!

This is truly the miracle that is freely available to all. And we are that miracle. There is no separation - there never was.

This is not some "special" state, this is not something that I have "attained"; no, this is true for each and every one of us. For all of us, the world appears for free, out of nothing, now, now and now. This requires no belief, no effort, no choice. It simply is.

This is it - this is what we've been searching for our whole lives. But we've not found it. If anything, the search has been seen through. By no-one.

Ah, words complicate. This is always so simple.

Into The Void

And so we come to the end of all things, which is really the beginning of all things. And at last the obvious reveals itself: there is only love, only this wide open space which welcomes everything, literally everything.

And it has *always* been this way, we've just been running round like headless chickens our whole lives trying to find it.

Only love, only unconditional acceptance as the essence and ground and condition of all things, although there is nobody here who could grasp what any of that means. If anything, the grasping which drove an entire lifetime's search has been seen through, and what is revealed is what was always present, throughout the entire search, literally right here: this, the undeniable present appearance of it all, the wide open space in which the entire world appears, all of it, without remainder. The seeking implied that there was something other than the entire world appearing now. Well, it was a nice game, a nice way to pass the time. But it was ultimately futile, for this is all there is, and all there ever was.

And this open space rejects nothing. Only a self would reject, indeed the self (that is, "you") is nothing but a rejection, a seeking for permanence, a denial of the reality that presents itself now, now and now. Only a self would seek, and in that seeking perpetuate its own existence. And only a self would seek the end of seeking, and in that, exaggerate itself, make itself stronger.

But this open space accepts all of that, too. Indeed, this open space is that which allows the entire world to be in the first place, as the philosophers have seen: no consciousness, no world. No me, no life. I am that very life, I cannot separate myself from it. I am what arises now, I am this, and this, and this too. Indeed, that very separation is what creates me as I know myself and as I experience myself. I am that very separation I seek to be free from. It's a vicious circle, and there's no escape.

But perhaps there is an escape (ah, words will never capture it!). And the escape is this, here, now. Already there is a world appearing for free, in each and every moment, asking nothing of you, not even asking for a "you" to come into being in the first place. Indeed, the "you" simply appears, or not, as part of the landscape, part of the texture of this moment.

Any spiritual practice or therapy in which we are supposed to transcend this "ego" simply perpetuates the very disease it purports to cure, because already, as the Buddhists have seen, this ego is simply an illusion in the sense that it is simply a bundle of thought arising now, through which the entire apparent world is perceived.

No self-transcendence is required, although please go down that path if you want to. Because already the individual who would go down that path, or indeed do anything at all, is simply a story, a belief arising now.

Life, but nobody here who lives it.

Life, with or without the heavy burden of "me and my problems".

Life, without a centre.

And so here the journey of a lifetime ends. The eyes grow weary, and sleep beckons. This day has been a dream, nothing more, nothing less, and not just this day, but all days: *all is dream.* This entire human life is nothing more than an elaborate and often convincing play of consciousness, a cosmic entertainment.

Everything arises, does its little dance, and dissolves back into the nothingness that I am in my essence, and I remain untouched by any of it. I am an open space in which a world is allowed to arise, again and again and again. I am not here, and yet I am fully immersed in the world. I don't care what happens, *I simply don't care.* And yet, *I care absolutely*, because I am not separate from any of it.

And so to bed. Another day has passed, and yet nothing has happened at all.

And the eyes close, and the world dissolves once again...

Goodnight.

Sunrise

And the eyes open. Again, the miracle: a world appears out of the void. A pointless world, a purposeless world, and yet still it appears!

The search is over: this present moment is the Answer of all Answers. The spiritual search, the search of a lifetime, is no more.

Nothing more needs to be done.

Well, that's not true at all.

There is lots to do: get up, shower, make breakfast, read the paper, go for a walk, meet up with friends. Chop wood and carry water.

Nothing to do, and yet an entire world presents itself now, now and now. And yes, it may be just an *apparent* world, but nonduality is not about denying anything.

So live your life, even though it is just an apparent life, even though you swim in a sea of Nothingness, even though it's all an illusion with nobody there at the centre of it all.

Live your life, you might as well. It's all the great play, the wonderful cosmic game. Everything is spiritual in this game: seeking the source of the "I" as much as having a beer down the pub, "being present" as much as wetting the bed at night when you're ninety years old and your bladder is packing in.

Everything is Empty, and so everything is divine.

Everything is illusion, and so everything matters absolutely.

Everything is simply an appearance, and so everything touches the heart in unimaginable ways, day after precious day.

And the search of a lifetime only ever brought us back here, to this moment, in order to read these words pointing to the utter futility of the search.

There is no such thing as enlightenment.

There is no such thing as liberation.

There is no such thing as awakening, there is no such thing as an awakened state, there are no awakened individuals.

There is only ever this – what is presently happening. And stories about awakening and liberation and enlightenment may arise in this, but they are only ever stories, and have no deeper reality.

But please, don't take my word for it. Go, and search if you want to. Search and search and search until you're blue in the face. And meditate, and self-enquire, and seek the root of the "I", and watch your breathing, and practise yoga, and undergo years and years of psychotherapy, and try to become more present, and think positively, and attempt to "manifest your destiny", and eat vegetarian food, and move to India and worship a guru, and have wonderful spiritual experiences, and discover "ultimate truths" about the universe, and reach enlightenment, and go round telling everyone you're enlightened, and that they can become enlightened too if they follow the same path.

And do all those things, and believe as many stories as you want to, and separate yourself from life in a billion different ways, and maintain and strengthen the very ego which you want to be free from.

Yes, do anything you like, experience whatever you want to experience, experience everything the world has to offer.

But all experiences pass. Nothing lasts, and *whatever* has apparently happened in the past, we are only ever left with this present appearance, arising right now. Whatever story is told about you and your wonderful life and your desperate search for liberation, it is only ever a story arising now. A story that already arises for no-one!

How terrifying this is to a mind seeking something more! It's the last thing we want to hear: there is only ever this present appearance, and the past is always dead and gone, and the awakening sought for an entire life-time was never something that could be found.

And you don't need to read any more books or go to any more meetings in order to "get" this, because, of course, there is nothing to get. But if the reading of books happens, and travelling to meetings happens, and meditation or self-enquiry happens, that's fine, that's wonderful, that's what is. Because *already* there is nobody who does any of these things anyway. Which is great news: there is nothing more that needs to be done. Really, honestly, nothing. The search is over.

And so, where does this leave us?

Right here:

The beating of the heart.

Breathing. In, out. In, out.

The radiator creaking.

The television buzzing.

Thoughts. Arising, dissolving. Arising, dissolving.

The story of "me and my life".

Hunger arising.

Pain in the back.

The phone ringing: your father loves you and misses you and wants to hear your voice...

Nothing special. Totally ordinary. And yet, completely and utterly extraordinary, because it is quite literally all there is.

You see, the search lied: it claimed that life was a problem and that escape was a possibility.

But there is no escape, and life is not a problem, and the search never happened in the first place.

The Secret

What a miracle it is to be alive right now, on this new day, on this day of all days! What a gift, what indescribable joy! To eat breakfast. To go to the toilet. To shower. To put on clothes. To walk out into the fresh air. To experience pain and pleasure, happiness and sadness, *even though* it's all a play of consciousness, *even though* everything happens for nobody...

To live, even though life is not separate from death. To move about this beautiful, fragile, transitory world, to meet yourself again and again in a thousand different places, to enjoy everything that life has to offer, even though you know you will eventually die; even though this body will be ravaged by cancer, or the heart will fail, or the limbs will be mangled beyond all recognition in a car accident...

To love others with all your heart and all your soul and all your might, to love them without conditions, to love them fiercely, passionately, to love them until it hurts, even though you know they will all die, all of them, every single one...

To go on, to insist on *life* and nothing less, even though every experience you ever had will fade into Nothingness, even though one day you will struggle to remember if any of it really happened at all...

Yes, at last, here's the secret: *this moment is life's only meaning.*

The birds have vanished into the sky,
and now the last cloud drains away.
We sit together, the mountain and me,
until only the mountain remains.

- Li Po

Further titles from NON-DUALITY PRESS

Printed in the United Kingdom
by Lightning Source UK Ltd.
132738UK00001B/75/A

9 780955 399978